Contents

Introduction

THE RIVERSIDES WAY is a 72 mile circular walk in that area of the Welsh Marches immediately to the south and west of Ludlow. (The word 'March' simply means a border or boundary.) The route was planned, walked and written up over a period of eighteen months between December 1998, as I was completing the initial draft of my first book – *The Elan Valley Way*, and May 2000. In many respects the new walk was an antidote to the routing restrictions of its predecessor. With the Elan Valley Way I had set myself the constraint of not straying more than three miles from the route of the aqueduct from mid Wales to Birmingham while also trying to avoid using 'A' or 'B' roads. With the new walk the 'A' and 'B' road constraint remained but apart from that my only consideration as to route was as regards suitable stage endings. Otherwise I was free to wander where I chose through what has become, over many years, my favourite walking area.

While others sing the praises of the Lake District, Yorkshire Dales or Scotland, for me the answer to the question of my preferred part of Britain in which to walk has always been that area within a circle of about a 30 mile radius around Ludlow. It includes the Abberley Hills of Worcestershire – much beloved of my childhood and youth – and a section of the Welsh Marches with many excellent walking bases such as Clun, Knighton, Bleddfa, Llangynllo, Leintwardine and Ludlow itself. It is an area of rolling hills where the counties of Herefordshire, Powys, Shropshire and Worcestershire meet. Above all, it is an secret place, still largely overlooked by the scores of trippers who flock to the 'honey pots' of Windermere, Grasmere or Grassington.

I have walked the area for as long as I care to remember but it was not until the past five years or so that I discovered a particularly secret part of this largely overlooked region – that to the immediate south and west of Ludlow. Perhaps the attractions of the town itself had caused me to overlook the jewel on its doorstep or was it that I was always *en route* to mid Wales when I passed through it? Either way, I eventually came across Aymestrey and the Lugg Valley one unforgettable late summer evening – when the sun had gone and the first chills of a coming autumn had caused one or two fires to be lit. I dropped down to the settlement in fading light, through woodland, with wood smoke hanging in the trees and the river murmuring below. A dog barked across the valley but no other living thing stirred. I could have been alone in the world for all I knew. As I crossed the last field before reaching the unusually quiet A4110 road I wondered what my accommodation in this new destination would be like. The Riverside Inn was as special as the rest of that first entrance into Aymestrey. It was welcoming, comfortable and immediately as familiar as an old friend. And every return to the inn and to Aymestrey since has been like a homecoming!

The walk in part takes its name from the inn. It is 'Riversides' rather than 'Riverside' because it takes in the valleys and surrounding hills of the two rivers that drain the region – the Teme, in the north, and the Lugg, in the south. Both are secretive, beautiful rivers. The lower Teme was familiar to me from my Worcester childhood – it joins the River Severn to the south of the city – and from my forays around the Abberley Hills. In its upper reaches it flows past settlements steeped in history – Knucklas, Knighton, Leintwardine and Ludlow – and through secret places, such as Downton Gorge. It is one of the fastest flowing rivers in the country. The Lugg is also swift flowing. It is also very clear, pacing through few settlements of any size in its upper reaches other than Presteigne. Its name means 'Clear Water'. Like the Teme at Downton Gorge the Lugg also imposed itself on the landscape of the area after the last Ice Age, cutting its own Gorge at Aymestrey.

The area covered by the walk is rich in human history. The hill fort at Croft Ambrey was first occupied over 2500 years ago. The A4110 at Aymestrey follows the course of a Roman road. The Saxon settlement that became Leintwardine is built on top of a Roman garrison town. Knucklas has its Arthurian legends. From Wigmore Queen Ethelfreda, daughter of Alfred the Great, defied the Danes. There are important Norman castle sites such as Richards Castle and Ludlow. There are churches which can trace their origins back to Saxon times, their sites to the Celts. Perhaps surprisingly there were also early outposts of the Industrial Revolution hereabouts – such as at Bringewood Forge.

At times the events which unfolded in the area were of national importance – the Welsh rising of Owain Glyn Dwr in the early fifteenth century, the Battle of Mortimer's Cross (1461), and the hundred years or so when the Mortimers of Wigmore and Ludlow Castles were at their most powerful, ruling the Marches and challenging both the authority and the legitimacy of the Crown.

Finally there is Ludlow – perhaps the most perfect of English towns. The book includes a Town Trail for those who would explore it. I still find something new at every visit.

I wrote, above, that the only constraint I felt under when designing the route of the Riversides Way was to avoid prolonged walking on 'A' or 'B' roads. That is not completely true because before I planned the route I decided upon the stage endings and here I was guided by Steve Bowen (of the Riverside Inn) as far as to whether he would be prepared to ferry walkers staying at the inn out to the points I had selected – a service he has long provided for guests walking the Mortimer Trail (Ludlow to Kington). He kindly agreed to my suggestions.

Many of the people who were involved when I was writing the 'Elan Valley Way' again helped with the new walk. Much of it was again walked with Alan Jones, who had obviously not been put off by the earlier venture and whose company lifts the spirits even in the darkest of walking moments! Fortunately these proved to be rare on the Riversides Way and even the weather smiled on us, unlike during our expeditions to the Elan Valley. Special thanks must also go to Val and Steve Bowen and all their staff at the Riverside Inn for their help, support, encouragement and welcome while I was working on the book. I hope that in some small way its contents will repay them.

I have split the 72 miles of the Riversides Way into eight stages, keeping these reasonably short – (the longest is 13 miles) – because of the limited public transport and accommodation options at some points on the route. I have deliberately limited the length of the Ludlow to Richards Castle stage so that it can be completed in conjunction with the Ludlow Town Trail. A short road link from Lower Lye to Aymestrey means that the 72 mile circular walk can be split into two separate circular walks – of about 40 and 36 miles – if so wished (see page 59).

There are separate sections covering Public Transport and Accommodation elsewhere in the book. As regards Public Transport I have tried to give as accurate a picture as possible of the situation which existed at the time of publication but the information should always be checked for accuracy before setting out. Rural Public Transport in Britain is sadly under funded and often poorly integrated. Changes to routes and timetables often happen at short notice. To help the prospective traveller I have given a list of 'useful' telephone numbers of Public Transport providers and the County Council information services. Similarly, in an area of variable and changing accommodation availability, I have provided the numbers of the relevant Tourist Information offices. Of course there is always the option – as long as it remains available – of staying at the Riverside Inn and being transported along the route as necessary.

The walk is suitable for undertaking at any time of the year. It should cause no problems for the fairly fit, experienced walker. The steepest climbs are mercifully fairly short! All paths on the route were passable at the time of publication with one very minor exception on Stage 1 which I have dealt with by leaving it as an 'option' and describing an alternative route in the main text. As far as I can ascertain all of the route is either over Public Rights of Way or areas of Open Access. Please remember to follow the Country Code and respect the land and its people – and hopefully you will reap what you sow!

Finally – the usual warning – in a publication of this nature the odd mistake is bound to occur and also changes which affect its accuracy may arise. I apologise in advance for the former; the latter we all must live with. I hope any problem the reader/walker might encounter does not spoil the enjoyment of the walk.

David Milton, Sheldon, Birmingham, 2001

Riversides Way - Mileages

	Total	
	0	Riverside Inn, AYMESTREY
2.5	2.5	Lyepole Bridge
2.5	5	Kinsham Church
4.5	9.5	PRESTEIGNE (end of Stage 1)
6.5	16	Cascob
2.5	18.5	BLEDDFA (end of Stage 2)
2.25	20.75	Llangynllo (Llangunllo)
5.25	26	KNIGHTON (end of Stage 3)
4	30	Powys Observatory
2	32	Willey Chapel
3	35	LINGEN (end of Stage 4)
3	38	Lower Lye
2	40	Wigmore
4.5	44.5	Adforton
3.5	48	LEINTWARDINE (end of Stage 5)
4.5	52.5	Bringewood Forge Bridge
2	54.5	Bromfield
3	57.5	LUDLOW (end of Stage 6)
3.75	61.25	Ashford Carbonel
0.75	62	Ashford Bowdler
2	64	RICHARDS CASTLE (end of Stage 7)
3	67	Orleton Common
5	72	Riverside Inn, AYMESTREY (end of Stage 8)

The Stage Maps

The entire route is covered by stage maps – either one or two per stage of the walk. The numbers which appear along the route on these relate to the same numbers within the main text.

The maps are not strictly drawn to scale but are generally at a scale of about 1½ inches to 1 mile. I have expanded this scale where the amount of detailed information to be shown requires this.

The maps are in no way intended to be a substitute for the Ordnance Survey maps of the route which should always be carried when undertaking the walk.

Ordnance Survey Maps covering the walk

1:50000 (Landranger): 137 Ludlow

1:25000 (Explorer): 201 Knighton & Presteigne; 203 Ludlow

Public Transport

The following is an overview of the situation as regards public transport at the stage endings (at the time of publication):

AYMESTREY: Bus Service 489 (Lugg Valley Primrose Travel) Leintwardine-Leominster. One bus each way daily, Monday to Friday only.

PRESTEIGNE: Bus Service 467/468 (Sargeants Brothers) To/From Knighton. Five buses each way daily, Monday to Saturday only. Bus Service 493/494 (Lugg Valley Primrose Travel) To/From Leominster. One bus each way on Friday only; two on Saturday.

BLEDDFA: Bus service (Owens Motors) To/From Knighton and Llangynllo. Two buses daily, Monday to Saturday.

KNIGHTON: Rail Service via Knighton Station on Heart of Wales Line. Swansea to Shrewsbury, for onward connections. (Wales & Borders Trains) Four trains each way daily Monday to Saturday. One train each way on Sunday during period of summer timetable only. Bus Service 738-740 (Shropshire Link) To Ludlow via Leintwardine and Bromfield. Five buses each way daily, Monday to Friday; four on Saturday.

LINGEN: No Public Transport available.

LEINTWARDINE: Bus Service 738-740 (Shropshire Link) Ludlow-Knighton. Five buses each way daily, Monday to Friday; four on Saturday. Bus Service 489 (Lugg Valley Primrose Travel) To/From Aymestrey and Leominster. One bus each way daily, Monday to Friday only.

LUDLOW: Rail Service via Ludlow Station on the main Manchester-Shrewsbury-Hereford-South Wales line. (Wales & Borders Trains) Regular daily service. Bus Service 192/292 Birmingham-Hereford. (Midland Red or Pete's Travel, on Sundays) Peak service of one bus each way per hour; less frequent off-peak; two buses each way on Sunday. Bus Service 738-740 (Shropshire Link) to Knighton via Bromfield and Leintwardine. Five buses each way daily, Monday to Friday; four on Saturday.

RICHARDS CASTLE: Bus Service 192/292 Birmingham-Hereford. (Midland Red or Pete's Travel, on Sundays) Peak service of a bus every two hours; less frequent off-peak; two buses each way on Sunday.

Details of public transport available at intermediate points are given in the text.

Useful Telephone Numbers

Herefordshire County Council: 01432 260948
Lugg Valley Primrose Travel: 01568 612759
Midland Red: 01905 763888
National Rail Enquiry Line: 08457 484950
Owen's Motors: 01547 528303
Pete's Travel: 0121 505 3245
Powys County Council: 01597 826642
Sargeants Brothers: 01544 230481
Shropshire Link: 01588 673113

The Riversides Way

Traveline (National Public Transport Information Service): 0870 6082608
Wales & Borders Trains: 0870 9000 772
Riverside Inn, Aymestrey: 01568 708440
Shropshire County Council: 01743 254036

Steve Bowen, at the Riverside Inn at Aymestrey, is prepared to transport anyone undertaking the Riversides Way and who is staying at the inn out to the start/finish points of the stages-subject to availability. Check beforehand when booking accommodation.

Accommodation

Stage 1

Aymestrey: Riverside Inn (01568 708440, Steve & Val Bowen). Otherwise limited. Contact Ludlow Tourist Information (01584 875053) or Leominster Tourist Information (01568 616460).
Presteigne: Contact Presteigne Tourist Information/Judge's Lodging (01544 260650).

Stage 2

Bleddfa: Hundred House Inn (01547 550333) is the only accommodation in Bleddfa. If full they may be able to advise regarding local farms offering accommodation. Otherwise use Knighton. Contact Knighton Tourist Information/Offa's Dyke Centre (01547 528753).

Stage 3

Knighton: Contact Knighton Tourist Information/Offa's Dyke Centre (01547 528753).

Stage 4

Lingen: No accommodation in Lingen. Contact Ludlow Tourist Information (01584 875053) or Leominster Tourist Information (01568 616460) regarding accommodation in surrounding area.

Stage 5

Leintwardine: Limited accommodation in Leintwardine. Contact Ludlow Tourist Information (01584 875053). Alternatively use Ludlow.

Stage 6

Ludlow: Contact Ludlow Tourist Information (01584 875053).

Stage 7

Richards Castle: Limited accommodation in Richards Castle. Contact Ludlow Tourist Information (01584 875053) or Leominster Tourist Information (01568 616460). Alternatively use Ludlow or Leominster.

Stage 8

Aymestrey: See under Stage 1.

About the Author

A RESIDENT of Birmingham for over 30 years now, David Milton was born in Worcester in 1949 and spent the first eighteen years of his life there before joining Customs & Excise, for whom he worked for almost thirty years, taking early retirement in 1997 to concentrate on his main interest – walking.

His interest in walking began young – sometime between five and ten years of age – with the Worcester & Birmingham Canal and Worcestershire's Abberley Hills providing early challenges. During the 1970s he walked almost the entire canal system of England and Wales and has since walked widely in Cornwall, the Derbyshire Peak District, the Lake District, Yorkshire, and the Cotswolds in the UK, and abroad in the Greek Islands, Malta, France, Madeira and India. His declared 'favourite' walking area however is that region around Ludlow where the counties of Herefordshire, Worcestershire, Radnorshire (Powys) and Shropshire mingle. The walk described in this book is very much the product of his many years of walking in this particular area.

His other interests include fossils, wildlife, canals, railways, steam locomotives, local history, maps and prints, travel, poetry, and music – especially American folk/blues. He is a dedicated 'non-driver'.

Since his retirement David has divided his time between walking for pleasure, leading walking groups – mainly in the Welsh Marches – and writing. The designer of many 'day walks', *The Riversides Way* is his second long distance walk and book. His first, *The Elan Valley Way*, was published by Meridian Books in 1999 and describes the route of a 128 mile walk from Birmingham to Mid-Wales based around the Elan Valley Aqueduct.

David is currently working on his third long distance walk and book – a route along the length of the River Teme, from Worcester to its source in the Kerry Hills of Mid Wales.

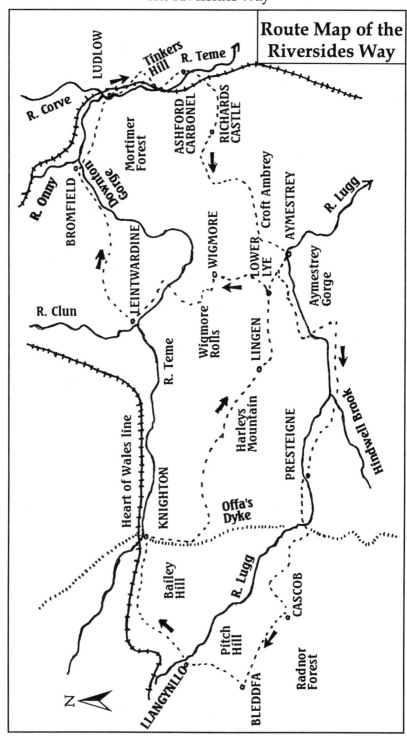

Route Map of the Riversides Way

Stage 1

Aymestrey to Presteigne

Mileage: 9½ Miles (From Aymestrey: 2½ miles to Lyepole Bridge;
5 miles to Kinsham Church)
O.S. Maps: 1:50000 (Landranger): 137 (Ludlow);
1:25000 (Explorer): 203 (Ludlow); 201 (Knighton & Presteigne)

*The route commences at the Riverside Inn at Aymestrey. Having crossed
the River Lugg it follows it westwards through Aymestrey Gorge to
Lyepole Bridge, via a quiet road and then a riverside track. Another quiet
road section takes the route up through Upper Lye and then an ancient
track, complete with legend, leads to Kinsham.*

*Dropping down through the grounds of Kinsham Court the route makes
its second crossing of the Lugg before following it past the settlement of
Byton. A short section of fieldpath walking takes it to the banks of the
river once more and the remainder of the stage sees the route follow first
the river, then its tributary – Hindwell Brook, and finally the Lugg again
to reach Presteigne.*

THE walk begins at the Riverside Inn, alongside Aymestrey Bridge
over the River Lugg, a lovely setting marred only by the noise of
traffic on the adjacent A4110 road. From the inn turn left to cross
the River Lugg via Aymestrey Bridge and walk along the A4110. Within
100 yards of the bridge take the first turning left, signposted 'The Mill,
Lingen' and 'Lye, Lingen', onto a quiet, narrow road. The first building
on the left along this is Aymestrey Mill.

*Aymestrey Mill was built in about 1800 on the site of a tenth century mill.
It was still in use for the production of flour until the mid 1960s and was
afterwards used to provide power for a print-making studio established in
converted stables adjoining it.*

Walk along the quiet road, the mill leat just over the hedge on the left
throughout and wooded slopes to the right. After about half a mile on
the road a weir will be seen in the Lugg down to the left, where the mill
leat leaves it. Remain on the road which continues straight ahead, still
with the wooded hill to the right and the river some fields distant to the
left. Further over to the left is Aymestrey Gorge.

*Walking this section I have often disturbed a heron fishing below the weir
while deer may sometimes be seen in the woodland to the right.*

The road makes a sharp bend to the left, near a point named as
'Sunnybank' on Explorer Map 203. Ignore a footpath going off the road

1

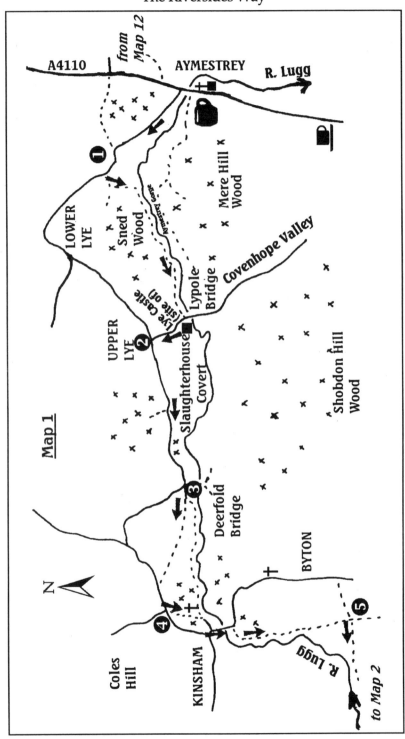

Map 1

The Riverside Inn

The building dates from 1580 and was constructed in the style of a Welsh longhouse – with accommodation for people at one end and for farm animals at the other, under one roof.

A flat site above the current building was formerly occupied by a small monastery which was later incorporated into the Abbey at Wigmore (see note at Stage 5).

In about 1700 the building became an inn – 'The Crown' – and in 1740 was extended to the rear. Two wooden seats dating from this period survive in the bar area.

The pub was owned by nearby Yatton Court until 1968 – being rented out as an inn with smallholding attached. In that year the inn was purchased as a distinct entity.

By the early 1990s the inn was in a somewhat run-down state. In 1994 it was purchased by Steve and Val Bowen who renamed it as 'The Riverside Inn' and have since built up its reputation as a restaurant. Still offering accommodation, the inn today also brews its own real ales – the actual brewery situated in the former outbuildings of a local farm (Woodhampton) which is passed on Stage 5 of the walk.

Like all buildings of its age and pedigree the Riverside is reputedly home to at least one ghost – in this instance a woman, possibly connected with water, who strokes the hands of unsuspecting guests.

Aymestrey

The settlement of Aymestrey lies just to the south of where the busy A4110 road – formerly the western arm of the Roman Watling Street – crosses the River Lugg.

There are two suggested sources for its name. The first is that it is derived from the dedication of its church, to Saint Alkmund of Mercia – a Christian Saxon leader who owned land at Lilleshall, Shropshire, and who was killed during the struggle against the Danes in the eighth century. Through the years the settlement name changed, from Alkmundstre through Aylmondistre and Aylmintre, to Aymestrey. The second suggested origin, again Saxon, is that the settlement name means 'Aepelmund's tree'. It appears as Elmodestreu in *Domesday Book* (1086).

Aymestrey church – unusually doubly dedicated, to St. John and St. Alkmund – is built on what is a presumed Saxon site. The dedication to St. Alkmund is thought to date from the time of Queen Ethelfreda, daughter of Alfred the Great, early in the tenth century. A series of churches dedicated to the same earlier Saxon warrior were built at this time to celebrate her own victories over the Danes.

The building seen today has a twelfth century Norman nave and chancel, with two surviving original windows in the north wall of the latter. The tower dates from the mid fourteenth century. Just below its parapet on the west (porch) side are two imposing gargoyles which drain rainwater from the roof. Inside, in the mid sixteenth century arcades were built using material from Wigmore Abbey – a victim of the dissolution of the monasteries under Henry VIII – the site of which is passed on Stage 5 of the walk. The woodwork of the rood screen is particularly fine and dates from about 1540 – again possibly originating elsewhere. The massive oak door to the building is medieval. In the porch are some fragments of lead from the church roof which bear the names of the churchwardens of 1749 when repairs were carried out.

Inside the church is the tomb of Sir John Lingen and his wife Elizabeth. Sir John fought for the Yorkist cause at the Battle of Mortimer's Cross (1461) – see page 6. The tomb is marked by an alabaster slab in the floor to the right of the altar on which the figures of the knight, in armour, and his lady are faintly incised. The tower of the church is crowned by a fine 'golden' weather-cock. In the churchyard is a fifteenth century Preacher's Cross.

In years past one of the six bells of the church was rung each evening to guide travellers through nearby Pokeshouse Wood to the safety of the village – a service paid for from the rent on a piece of land set aside for this purpose by some luckless person who had spent a long night lost in these thick woods to the east of the settlement. (The approach to Aymestrey down through the wood is today used by the main route of the waymarked Mortimer Trail and it is still dark and gloomy among the conifers there.)

The Yorkists used the church to stable horses before the Battle of Mortimer's Cross. Some of the battle dead are reputedly buried in a mass grave in the churchyard.

The bridge over the Lugg at the north end of the settlement looks to be of some age but in fact dates only from 1932. It replaced a narrower structure of similar design which itself had replaced a bridge destroyed by floods in 1795. A stone which formed part of the arch of the pre 1795 structure was recovered from the river bed and is incorporated in the parapet of the current bridge – as a metal plaque on the bridge explains.

Adjacent to river and bridge is the Riverside Inn – see separate note – while across both road and river from this is the striking Georgian building of Yatton Court.

The modern settlement of Aymestrey has a sub-post office/general store and a garden centre. There is a very limited bus service – (489 Leominster – Leintwardine; one bus daily each way, operated by Lugg Valley Primrose Travel) – through the village which stops outside the Riverside Inn. At the southern end of the village is a small tearoom, Village Teas, open daily from 10a.m. to 6p.m.

to the right here. A bend to the right follows, the road passing – on the right – the entrance drive to two dwellings, 'Squirreldene' and 'Number 2 Ballsgate'. The road then bends left, a small cottage just above it on the right hand side and a stream to the left. Opposite the cottage leave the road, left, as indicated by a Mortimer Trail signpost and following the arm of this marked 'Kington 16'. Cross a stile situated to the left of a metal farm gate (SO414665). **❶**

Follow the track which leads straight ahead from the farm gate up the field so entered. On nearing another metal farm gate, giving access to woodland, do not pass through it but instead leave the track, left, as indicated by a Mortimer Trail marker post. Walk about 40 yards, the boundary with the woodland immediately on the right, to reach a wooden gate with a stile to its left. Cross the stile onto a path which is followed through the length of Aymestrey Gorge.

Aymestrey Gorge is a riot of wildflowers in season. Walking here I have often seen heron and woodpeckers, occasionally deer. A beautiful section of riverside walking.

The steep wooded hill to the immediate right is Sned Wood while that across the river to the left is Mere Hill Wood.

Follow the path through the gorge. It is confined between the steep lower slopes of Sned Wood, on the right, and the boundary fence of riverside meadows, on the left, throughout. An initial gentle climb is followed by as gentle a descent and the path then levels out to pass through the gorge itself. As it proceeds through the gorge the path widens to track width.

Eventually the track passes an isolated cottage, on the left, and a wooden barrier designed to prevent vehicular access. Beyond these it reaches a junction with a road, Lyepole Bridge just to the left (SO398655).

To the left is the valley of Covenhope, probably the pre Ice Age course of the Lugg, before it cut Aymestrey Gorge. Ahead half-left Shobdon Hill Wood rises to a height of 326 metres/1066 feet.

Turn right up the quiet road which climbs steeply. As it bends to the right the rate of ascent lessens but then steepens again.

At a noticeable bend look left over a farm gate and into the river valley to see – beyond the bottom boundary of a field – the remains of the earthworks of Lye Castle, above the Lugg. The castle possibly dated from before the Norman Conquest.

At a road junction go left – signposted 'Limebrook, Lingen'. The road passes through the small farming settlement of Upper Lye, a telephone box on the left just after the junction. **❷**

The long upturned boat shape of Shobdon Hill Wood is now directly to the left across the Lugg valley.

Remain on the narrow road as it begins to wind and descend slightly. It passes an old half timbered longhouse dwelling, 'Bach Brook' (Small Brook) – on the left – crossing a stream and beginning to climb. Passing Western Lye Farm – on the left – it levels out, now some height above the Lugg valley to the left.

The small woodland to the left of the road just after Western Lye Farm is known as Slaughterhouse Covert. It is thought that its name commemorates the aftermath of the Battle of Mortimer's Cross (1461) – see note below – when remnants of the defeated Lancastrian force fled the battlefield along Covenhope valley but were caught hereabouts, either by the pursuing Yorkists or locals, and put to the sword.

Many of the Lancastrian force were men of Welsh descent who would have been particularly disliked locally because of the ongoing Welsh raids across the border into this part of Herefordshire over the years – it being only some sixty years since the Welsh uprising under Owain Glyn Dwr and with the battlefield of Pilleth (1402) the scene of a famous and particularly bloody Welsh victory, only a few miles further up the Lugg (see note at Stage 2).

The Battle of Mortimer's Cross

Just under two miles to the south of Aymestrey is the site of the Battle of Mortimer's Cross – a decisive moment in the Wars of the Roses. A Yorkist force, under Edward (Earl of March and son of Richard, Duke of York) defeated the Lancastrians, under Jasper Tudor (Earl of Pembroke) after a bloody battle on 3rd. February 1461. After the battle Edward was declared King of England (Edward IV) a position he consolidated by marching on London and eventually defeating a second Lancastrian force, under Queen Margaret, at Towton on 29th. March.

The Mortimer's Cross encounter was preceded by the appearance in the sky of a phenomenon known as a *parhelion*, or three suns, which was seized upon as an omen for coming victory by Edward – who later adopted the Sun in Splendour as his device/badge.

Some of the beaten Lancastrian force – many of them of Welsh origin – fled north-west from the slaughter, via Covenhope to the Lugg valley, only to be caught and massacred there. Slaughterhouse Covert – passed on Stage 1 of the walk – probably commemorates this. Estimates of the total number killed in the battle vary widely but a figure of anything up to 4000 is possible. Some are thought to be buried in a mass grave in Aymestrey churchyard.

A monument outside the Monument Inn at Kingsland, south of the battlefield, commemorates the battle, its aftermath and the triumph of Edward IV. Erected in 1799, it perpetuates an incorrect date, of 2nd. February, previously accepted as being that of the battle.

Look down through the trees here for glimpses of the Lugg in its valley far below. The prominent hill, wooded at the top, slightly to the right ahead is Cole's Hill (334 metres/1095 feet).

The road begins to descend through a narrow rocky cutting, bending right and then left. It drops to a road junction. Here go right, signposted 'Lingen'. *A short walk (200 yards) along the road going left at the junction – indicated as a No Through Road – brings one to a peaceful riverside setting at Deerfold Bridge.*

About 20 yards after the junction leave the road, left, onto a track to cross a stream (Lime Brook) via a footbridge to the left of a 'Private' bridge carrying the track and to the right of a ford (SO379654). Across the stream go straight ahead up a stony/gravelled track, a dwelling on the right (Lower Yeld). Where the gravelled track bends to the right to enter the grounds of the dwelling continue straight ahead on a dirt track to pass through a metal farm gate.

Ignore a path (Public Bridleway) which goes left immediately after the gate but continue straight ahead up the somewhat sunken dirt track, known locally as 'Dead Woman's Lane' (see box on page 8). ❸

When the track loses its sunken nature keep immediately alongside the boundary hedge on the right, the way still obvious underfoot. As the track underfoot becomes less distinct keep to the edge of a depression in the ground alongside the boundary fence on the right (presumably the old sunken track) while heading through a field. Reaching the far side of this field pass through a metal farm gate.

The River Lugg

The Lugg rises in the hills of Powys – on the slopes of Pool Hill, to the north-west of Llangynllo (Llangunllo). From there it flows south-east through Presteigne and then east to pass through Aymestrey Gorge, after which it turns south and then south-east again to reach Leominster where it is joined by its main tributary, the River Arrow. It then heads south to join the River Wye just to the east of Hereford.

Another sizeable tributary of the Lugg is Hindwell Brook, the confluence with which will be seen later on this stage of the walk, east of Presteigne.

It is thought that prior to the last Ice Age the Lugg flowed due south from Lyepole Bridge along the valley now known as Covenhope. When this was blocked by glacial activity the build-up of water finally broke through to the east, carving out what is now known as Aymestrey Gorge to give the drainage pattern as seen today.

The name 'Lugg' is derived from the Welsh 'Llugwy' meaning 'Clear Wye', the name 'Wye' itself being from the Celtic 'Wy' and signifying water.

The Riversides Way

The small settlement of Limebrook is visible over to the right while even further over in this direction may be seen the rounded summit of Harley's Mountain, crossed on Stage 4 of the Riversides Way. Cole's Hill is ahead right.

Through the gate, go straight ahead through a long narrow field towards a metal farm gate which will be seen in the distance ahead. On reaching the far end of the field go straight ahead along a track and through the aforementioned farm gate. Continue along the track which eventually reaches a junction with a road. Turn left along this.

On reaching the road pause and look behind for superb views down the Lugg valley, with the hills around it – Shobdon Hill Wood, Mere Hill Wood and Sned Wood – with Yatton Hill (seen at closer quarters on Stage 8 of the walk) visible through the gap of Aymestrey Gorge on the far horizon.

Not many yards along the road the name-sign for Kinsham is passed and, soon afterwards, the first few dwellings of the settlement. At a junction ignore a road going right – indicated as a No Through Road. Only about 15 yards beyond this junction leave the road, left, for a public footpath via a kissing gate (SO364651). ❹

The path descends and almost immediately crosses a stream via a wooden footbridge. Over this, go slightly right downhill on an indistinct track, following overhead power lines and poles. On the left are outbuildings and houses belonging to the Kinsham Court estate. Aim to the right of the bottom of the overhead power poles, buildings to the left, ignoring a track which goes half-right here. Beyond the pole

---

Dead Woman's Lane

This is the subject of local legend. Apparently, at the end of the nineteenth century it was decided to close Kinsham churchyard to burials. This meant that corpses from the settlement would have to be taken north over the hill to Lingen for burial instead. The first death after the closure was early one January and was that of an old lady. A funeral service was held in Kinsham church and then a procession, headed by coffin bearers, set off up the hill for Lingen. Before long the weather closed in and a snowstorm started and this, plus the temptations of a wake to attend, soon resulted in members of the procession drifting away back down the hill to Kinsham until only the four coffin-bearers were left with their burden.

On reaching the brow of the hill, where the sunken track now meets the road, the storm became really bad whereupon the bearers decided to abandon the coffin in a convenient hut and go to the wake, the intention being to collect the coffin for burial later. The story goes that such a good time was had by all at the wake that afterwards the coffin was completely forgotten and remained in the hut until its discovery in the Spring. At least this is the legend! (*My thanks to Zog, North Herefordshire Footpath Warden, for this story.*)

head towards a large wellingtonia tree to locate a stile which is situated immediately to the left of it. Over the stile, drop down to cross the metalled drive to Kinsham Court, bearing slightly left across it – the house to the left – to walk along a track opposite, on the edge of woodland (right) and with the garden of the house on the left.

On reaching the corner of a paddock – with wooden fence and gate ahead – bear slightly right around its corner to walk along the outside of its fence (left).

To visit the small church of All Saints, Kinsham, bear left instead of right on reaching the paddock corner where a path climbs between the paddock (right) and the garden of the house (left) to enter the churchyard at its west side.

The rather drab, mainly pebble dash exterior of this simple single-chambered building masks a structure of some age. The church dates from the late thirteenth century but there is a suggestion that a window in the south wall may be older still. Inside is a monument to Thomas Harley (died 1738) of the local landowning family and also coats of arms of both the Harley and Mortimer families. The graveyard contains some interesting and attractive headstones from the eighteenth and nineteenth centuries.

The adjacent Kinsham Court dates from the late seventeenth century but incorporates remains of an older fourteenth and fifteenth century building.

Returning to the main route after visiting the church one May morning we surprised a deer which panicked and became trapped in the paddock outside until, fearing capture was imminent, it cleared the wooden boundary fence with some ease.

Continue along the outside of the paddock fence until reaching a wooden gate in it. Here bear right, away from the fence, to drop down into woodland. The path widens to track width, a stream alongside it in a small valley on the right as it bends left and drops deeper into the woods. On reaching stream level, at the edge of the wood, the track meets a narrow metalled road. Turn right along this, almost immediately crossing the stream which accompanied the descent through the woods.

Across the meadows to the left may be seen the River Lugg. The long upturned boat shaped wooded hill ahead left is Wapley Hill.

On reaching a minor road junction turn left. The road soon crosses the Lugg via a metal road bridge. *The simple iron bridge bears the name and location of its makers – R. Masefield of Chelsea – and is one of several similar structures over both Lugg and Teme in this part of Herefordshire. Currently the subject of a weight restriction, it is due to be strengthened or replaced.*

About 35 yards beyond the bridge the road bends left and climbs. Here leave it, right, through a metal farm gate and onto a footpath.

Go straight ahead from the metal gate, beneath trees, the river about 35 yards away on the right. Follow the obvious path/track through the trees. It soon bears left, following a bend in the river. At a staggered 'crossroads' of tracks go straight on, as indicated by footpath signs on trees (ie. remain on a level; do not climb). The river is now somewhat nearer on the right.

The path/track eventually reaches the very river's edge.

A delightful section of riverside walking follows, with masses of bluebells hereabouts in season.

Continuing to follow the riverside path cross a stile. Bear slightly left from this, away from the river, to cross a wooden footbridge over a side stream. Climb up the low bank ahead to walk along the right edge of a field, above the river. Follow the edge of the field and on reaching its corner round this, to the left, to walk up its far boundary for about 30 yards. Here locate a wooden footbridge across a small stream down to the right. Cross the bridge into the next field and go straight ahead across the field, heading for a single large tree in the opposite boundary. Cross a stile just to the right of the tree and continue in the same direction across the next field, now heading directly for the large rounded mass of Wapley Hill.

Crossing these fields, the small settlement in view over to the left, below the slopes of Shobdon Hill Wood, is Byton. Visible to the left of the settlement is the church of St. Mary. On a religious site dating back over 1000 years the present church here was rebuilt in 1859 after a stove fire two years previously, the village raising £740 – a not inconsiderable sum in those days – as a half-share of the cost. A church on the same site had previously been sacked and burned by Owain Glyn Dwr in 1406. A carved stone lintel or tympanum (Agnus Dei, or Lamb and Cross), now set in the south wall of the building, dates from about 1100 as does the font inside.

The right hand boundary fence of the field is initially some distance away but this reduces as progress is made. Nearing the far side of the field, and maintaining direction, walk alongside the fence to reach a metal farm gate in it (SO366637). There is a 'crossroads' of footpaths at this point. **5**

Turn right to pass through the metal farm gate into the adjacent field. From the gate head half-right across the new field (parallel to the slopes of Wapley Hill on the left) towards another gateway which will be seen ahead. Pass through the gateway (gate likely to be open) into the next field. Go straight ahead across this large field to eventually reach a wooden footbridge over a stream. Crossing this go straight ahead to a stile/footbridge leading into the corner of an adjacent field, a farm gate to its right. Cross the stile/footbridge and follow the right hand boundary of the field to reach the banks of the Lugg.

Glorious views of Byton and Shobdon Hill Wood behind, on reaching the river.

Reaching the river at a bend, continue straight ahead – NOT along the riverbank – towards another bend in it. On reaching this locate a stile, ahead, over the next field boundary and cross this.

The river banks hereabouts are a favourite haunt of sand martins which may be seen swooping low over the water in season.

Initially follow the right hand boundary through the next field, an abandoned loop of the river immediately on the right. Where the boundary and river veer away to the right maintain direction across the field to reach a stile in the boundary ahead. Cross this into the next field. Initially maintain the same direction through this field, heading towards a pole carrying overhead lines which stands alongside an abandoned loop of the river.

A second pole on the opposite side of the Lugg was in imminent danger of being washed away when we walked this way after heavy April rains.

Crossing these fields, Wapley Hill is on the left and Cole's Hill on the right across the river. The wooded hill now becoming visible directly ahead bears Cann and Nash Woods and lies immediately south of Presteigne.

On reaching the pole maintain direction across the remainder of the field to locate a stile over its far boundary. Cross this into the next field. From the stile go straight ahead across the field to eventually meet the riverbank again. Continue along this, passing the confluence of the Lugg and the Hindwell Brook *en route*, the waterside walk now following the banks of the latter.

The boundary between England (Herefordshire) and Wales (Powys) flirts with both Lugg and Hindwell Brook hereabouts and can get very convoluted indeed in places. A short distance upstream on the Lugg from the confluence is Rosser's Bridge where the boundary is such that the Bridge is in Wales but most of the land on either side of it is England! The Riversides Way stays firmly in Herefordshire for the present, as it has been since Aymestrey.

Continue to follow the path along the bank of Hindwell Brook, through the remainder of the field, to reach a stile. Cross this into the next field and again follow the brook.

The highest part of the long mass of Wapley Hill is now directly to the left. Rising to 329 metres/1079 feet in height the summit bears an Iron Age hill fort covering 25 acres, one of many in this area which have been suggested as being the site of the last stand of the British leader Caractacus against the Roman legions of Scapula (AD51). It has a better claim than many for this honour.

On reaching the next field boundary cross another stile. Continue to follow the waterside path through the new field until reaching a fence. Walk left along this to reach a metal farm gate in the corner of the field.

Pass through this onto a track and follow this to a junction with a fairly busy road – the B4362. **❻**

As we crossed the last field before the B4362 one May afternoon, a curlew flew overhead and then proceeded to serenade us from a field across Hindwell Brook.

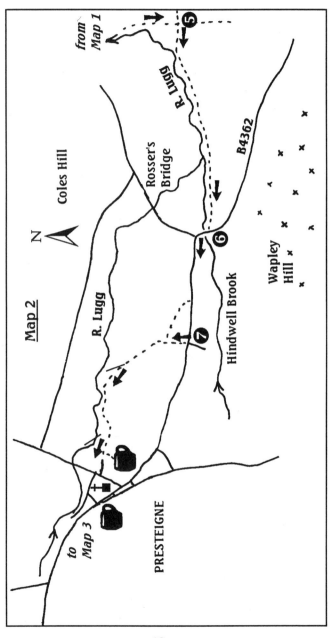

Aymestrey to Presteigne

Turn right along the road. Almost immediately it crosses Hindwell Brook via a low stone bridge. At a junction ignore a road going right, signposted 'Kinsham 1, Lingen 3', but remain on the B road which, fortunately has fairly wide verges.

Walking along the road, the premises of Presteigne Gates are passed on the left – the source of many of the metal farm gates which will be seen throughout the length of the Riversides Way. The adjacent house has rather magnificent rearing stallions on its gateposts and also bears an equine weathervane.

Just beyond these premises the road, and Riversides Way, leaves Herefordshire (England) to enter Powys (Wales).

Continue along the B road. Just after a bend to the left in it there is an old milestone on the verge on the right and just beyond this a track joins the road from the left. A footpath should leave the road, right, opposite this but at the time of writing there was no sign of a stile over the field boundary fence here (SO339637).

(Option: A few yards further along the road it is possible to climb over an old metal gate on the right into the field. If taking this option then on entering the field bear half-left to walk through it, eventually reaching a boundary hedge – that opposite the road as the field is first entered – and following this along to the far left corner of the field to climb over a similar metal farm gate and reach a track – see below. Then turn right along the track. Neither of the farm gates to the field is an easy climb so if not taking this option continue as below.)

The old milestone bears the distances to London – no longer decipherable – and Presteigne – '2 Miles' – and an Ordnance Survey bench mark.

At the end of a straight section of road after the milestone, as a slight bend right begins – and at the far end of the long field on the right – take a track (signed as a public footpath) which leaves the road, right, at SO334636. (Note: A metalled track leaves the road, left, at the same point and is signed as a byway Open to All Traffic.) **❼**

Walk along the track which is partly metalled initially and is bounded by the fence to the large field, on the right, and the garden boundary fences of two dwellings, on the left. The track soon loses its metalled surface and passes a metal farm gate into the field on the right over which the optional route (above) emerges.

On leaving the road for the track Cole's Hill is half-right ahead while the hill almost directly ahead is Stapleton Hill. Half-left is Hell Peak and Stapleton Wood, above Presteigne.

Continue to follow the now dirt track which continues between hedges to reach a metal farm gate with a stile alongside it to its left. Cross the stile into a large field and head half-left across it, aiming just to the right of the far left-hand corner. Here locate a stile/footbridge, about 40 yards in from the field corner, immediately to the right of a large ash tree.

Cross the stile/footbridge over a small stream into the next field. Here again bear half-left to its far left corner to find a stile situated on the bank of the River Lugg.

Cross the stile into the next field and follow the riverbank. Where the river bends sharply away to the right continue straight ahead across the large field until reaching the riverbank again, at the far side of the field. Here locate and cross a stile, just a few yards in from the riverbank, into the next field. Go straight ahead from the stile across the field, the river meandering on the right. At the far side of the field locate a stile about 35 yards in from the riverbank and cross it into the next field. The river should now be one field distant on the right.

The river here forms the border between Wales (Powys) to the south, and England (Herefordshire) to the north, across it.

Entering this latest field, the tower of Presteigne church comes into view ahead.

Bear slightly left, away from the hedge boundary on the right, from the stile to cross the field. Aim for a point about 20 yards to the right of the field's far left-hand corner to locate a stile in the boundary ahead. Cross the stile and then a wooden footbridge over a stream (Clatterbrook). Over the stream, follow the left-hand boundary through the new field – heading directly towards the tower of Presteigne church. On reaching a stile in the far corner of the field cross it to emerge onto a track. Follow the track, still heading towards the church tower. Ignore a footpath going left off the track.

Continue along the track. As it passes some new bungalows, on the right, it takes on a metalled surface. The resulting lane emerges onto a road in Presteigne (Broad Street) directly opposite an entrance to the churchyard. Cross the road and enter the churchyard. Immediately bear left on a path which runs around the left-hand side of the church to reach its tower porch where this stage of the Riversides Way ends.

On reaching the road in Presteigne turn left for the centre of the town or right for the Lugg Bridge which marks the border between Wales and England.

Presteigne

Its position on the borders of Wales and England has meant that Presteigne – its Welsh name is Llanandras (the church of St. Andrew) – has had a turbulent history. Its original name was Presthemede which probably means 'priest-household' and its origins can be traced back to a group of Saxon priests who built a small church here and settled near to a natural crossing point of the River Lugg in the late tenth or early eleventh century. In 1052 the surrounding district was ravaged by the Welsh leader Gruffyd ap Llywelyn which is probably the reason the settlement is not mentioned in *Domesday Book* (1086).

In the late twelfth century a second small settlement was founded around a newly built castle on the Warden, to the south of the present town, and the two settlements soon merged to form the present small market town.

During the thirteenth century it was attacked by the Welsh under Llywelyn the Great and was again sacked by Owain Glyn Dwr in the early years of the fifteenth century. These continuing Welsh incursions coupled with the effects of the Black Death in the area in the late fourteenth century meant that the fortunes of the town stagnated for a period.

During most of the Middle Ages the town was in the possession of the Mortimers of Wigmore and later Ludlow castles, the powerful dynasty of Marcher Earls who dominated English history at this time and whose successor became king, as Edward IV, after the battle of Mortimers Cross in 1461.

By the middle of the sixteenth century the town was once more thriving as a market centre, with a well established cloth manufacturing industry. By the middle of the seventeenth century it had taken over from Rhayader as the county town and County Assizes centre for Radnorshire. As the London to Aberystwyth road passed through the town it had also become an important route/coaching centre.

This point marked the peak in the town's fortunes. The cloth industry was in decline by the mid seventeenth century and local prosperity suffered further when the London to Aberystwyth stage coach was re-routed through Kington in the 1820s. Knighton gradually replaced it as the main local market centre and by the nineteenth century it relied solely on its Assizes and status as county town. In 1884 this last role was lost to the rapidly growing Llandrindod Wells. The last Assizes were held in the town in October 1970.

Probably the most significant building in the town is the church of Saint Andrew, where this stage of the Riversides Way ends. There has been a church on this site since Saxon times – see above. The present building dates largely from the fourteenth century but contains vestiges of both the original Saxon and a later Norman building. A stone over the east window of the church is inscribed 'M.P.L.1244' which is thought to stand for the Latin words meaning 'Mortimer was pleased to erect'. The porch-tower was added in the fifteenth century in front of the south doorway, the tower previously being detached from the main body of the church.

Inside the church, the font dates from the fourteenth century. At the foot of a pillar nearby is an ancient stone bowl found near Stapleton Castle, to the north of the town, which is thought to date from the early thirteenth century. In the north wall of the nave is a low recess which contains a decorated stone coffin lid – with foliated cross – thought to date from about 1240.

On the south wall of church is a modern metal sculpture designed and made by Peter Smith, a local blacksmith, and used as a *pricket* or candle stand. It represents a world of misery and need portrayed through the images of the last moments of a mother and child in Rwanda. Its creator writes 'It was brought into my front room by a technology which spans the globe and flashes up images of the human condition which we would prefer to ignore. How many of you will choose to fiddle while Rome burns?'

Also within the church are two features unique in Great Britain. On the north wall of the nave hangs a framed large late medieval tapestry, woven in silk and wool and depicting Christ's entry into Jerusalem. It dates from about 1510 and until 1737 hung in the home of a local family, the Owens, being given to the church in that year. It was used as the church altarpiece until the nineteenth century. It has recently (1999) undergone specialist conservation work. In the clock chamber of the church tower is a working wooden carillon, powered by a system of weights and pulleys, which is controlled by the clock mechanism and can be set to play tunes on the eight church bells. It was installed in 1726.

Outside in the churchyard, opposite the porch-tower door is the grave of Mary Morgan, a local girl of sixteen who was hanged in 1805 for the murder of her baby. The headstone, erected by a friend of the trial judge, tells the story.

The entrance to the churchyard further to the south along Broad Street from that used by the Riversides Way was originally via a lychgate, a stone structure dating from 1710, but this was demolished in 1891. An oval stone tablet set in the wall is all that remains of it. It is inscribed *'Opus Joannis Robinson – Lignum inveni, Saxum reliqui An. 1710'* which roughly translates as 'The work of John Robinson, who in the year 1710 replaced a wooden structure with one of stone'. The entrance to the churchyard here is known as the Scallions, thought to be a corruption of the Norse 'skallwega' meaning 'the way of the skull'.

A curfew bell is still rung from the church each evening, a practice dating from 1565 when John Beddoes, a wealthy local cloth merchant made it a condition for the founding of a grammar school by him in the town. Further along Broad Street, to the north, is Lugg Bridge which dates from the seventeenth century.

The most popular tourist attraction in the town is the Judge's Lodging (Llety'r Barnwr), on Broad Street. The former Shire Hall, the building dates from 1829, cost £7000, and was the judicial centre for Radnorshire. After the last Assizes, in 1970, it was restored and re-opened as an award winning museum with an imaginative 'audiotour' included, which recreates the mid Victorian heyday of the building. The premises also include Presteigne's Tourist Information Centre from where a very informative Town Trail is available. Just along Broad Street from the Judge's Lodging is the Market Hall and Assembly Rooms, the Italianate tower of which dominates the town centre. It was built in 1865 at a cost of £1300.

The lesser buildings of the town centre are somewhat older than a first glance might suggest with many nineteenth century shop fronts concealing much earlier buildings of the sixteenth and seventeenth centuries, as in both Broad Street and High Street. In High Street a Georgian frontage hides the Manor House, the oldest house in the

Mary Morgan's grave, Presteigne churchyard

town which dates from the fifteenth century. Also in High Street note the crude and somewhat indistinct carving of a 'Green Man' on the left hand side of one of the timber brackets to Number 47.

The oldest inn in the town is the Duke's Arms in Broad Street and dates from the fifteenth century. It was renamed after the Duke of Chandos, an important local magnate, in the eighteenth century having previously been called the Talbot. It was the premier coaching inn of the town and home to the last and longest routed mail coach in the country. The Radnorshire Arms in High Street dates from 1616 although it did not become an inn until 1792.

The Mortimers built a stone castle on the Warden to the south of the town between 1160 and 1200. It was destroyed by the Welsh in 1262 and never rebuilt. The site was later presented to the town as an amenity and is now a public park and picnic area.

To the north of the town was Stapleton Castle. A wooden castle dating from the time of the Norman Conquest, it had been rebuilt in stone by the second half on the twelfth century. It was held by the le Scrob family, later the de Says, who also held Richard's Castle – see note at Stage 8 of the Riversides Way – and were rivals of the Mortimers in the area. In 1671 it passed into the hands of the Harley family of Brampton Bryan. It withstood sieges by Simon de Montfort (1263) and Owain Glyn Dwr (1401) in its time but gradually fell into disrepair after the Civil War. The castle site is reputedly haunted by a ghost known as Lady Bluefoot. There are two versions of her story. The first is that a servant at the castle fell in love with the Lady but when she did not respond drowned her husband in the River Lugg and then, still repulsed in his advances, murdered her – her ghost returning every year to haunt the site. The second version has the lady murdered by her husband who believed she had been unfaithful. Before she died she swore her innocence and said that white violets would bloom around the castle every Christmas as proof of this.

Modern Presteigne has all the facilities as befits a small country market town. It was formerly linked to the main railway system via the Titley Junction to Presteigne Railway which opened in 1875 and left the line between Kington and Leominster at Titley Junction. The line was never very successful and closed to passengers in 1951 and to freight in 1964.

Stage 2

Presteigne to Bleddfa

Mileage: 9 Miles
(From Presteigne: 6½ miles to Cascob)
O.S.Maps: 1:50000 (Landranger): 137 (Ludlow);
1:25000 (Explorer): 201 (Knighton & Presteigne)

Leaving Presteigne alongside the Withybeds & Wentes Meadow Nature Park and River Lugg the route soon crosses the river to follow a bridleway due west towards the hills of Radnor Forest. A second Lugg crossing is made in the company of Offa's Dyke Path before the route leaves that national trail behind to climb up into the northern reaches of the Forest via Litton Hill and the lower slopes of Llan-fawr. There are superb views to be had behind, down the Lugg valley and through the Presteigne Gap, as this climb proceeds.

Descending a sunken track the route next visits the secluded valley of the Cascob Brook and the small settlement of the same name with its interesting little church. It then climbs up to and through Forest Wood to begin a long descent into the small hamlet of Bleddfa.

S TARTING outside the entrance to the porch-tower of St. Andrew's church, facing away from the building, turn right to follow a path out of the churchyard.

On reaching the edge of the churchyard bear left along a street, as indicated by an information signpost arm pointing to 'Nature Trail & Picnic Area'. At a road junction bear right into West Wall. At a further road junction go right, again as indicated by the information signpost arm for the 'Nature Trail & Picnic Area', into Mill Lane.

Follow Mill Lane out of Presteigne, the River Lugg down to the right. Just before the lane peters out at an isolated dwelling – 'The Old Mill' – leave it, half-left, along a narrow path again signed for 'Nature Trail & Picnic Area'.

A few yards along the narrow path ignore another path going left up steps but continue straight ahead. On reaching a wooden kissing gate ignore a path going down steps to the right into the Withybeds Nature Park.

The Withybeds & Wentes Meadow Nature Park covers a total area of six acres and is managed by the Radnorshire Wildlife Trust. There is an information board regarding the site at the top of the steps by the kissing gate.

19

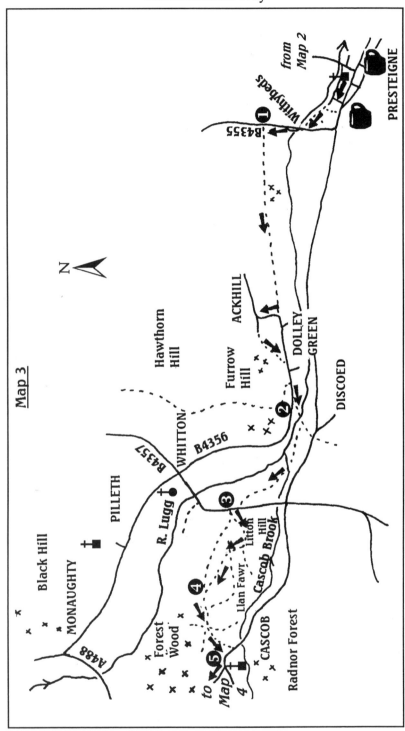

Map 3

Presteigne to Bleddfa

Pass through the kissing gate and continue straight ahead. Ignore a path going left up a bank and through another kissing gate into an adjacent field but continue ahead with the boundary fence of the nature reserve immediately on the right. Crossing a grassy area gradually bear left to reach a boundary fence on that side and then continue along this to reach a kissing gate in the far left-hand corner. Pass through this onto a fairly busy road – the B4355.

Turn right along the road, crossing it immediately. After only about 25 yards on the road leave it, left, along a metalled track which runs alongside a dwelling called 'Willowbrook'. The track crosses the Lugg via a stone bridge – Boultibrooke Bridge – with an attractive weir on the river just below it. It then rejoins the B4355. Turn left along this.

The road climbs gradually and begins a long bend to the left. The climb soon steepens. After about 260 yards on the road, with the climb and long bend still continuing, leave the road – left – through a metal farm gate and onto a track signed as a Public Bridleway (SO309656) (Note: The turning is about 50 yards before a former toll-house on the right of the road.) ❶

Go straight ahead from the gate along an obvious and quite sunken dirt track, the grounds of Oaklea Park down to the left. The track passes through a metal farm gate. Remain on it, a field fence on the right and open parkland with trees on the left.

Nice views down to the River Lugg in its valley on the left. Distant views of Presteigne over the left shoulder, behind.

The track passes through another gateway – (gate may be open) – with woodland obscuring the previous open views to the left and the field boundary still alongside on the right. Following the edge of the woodland it begins to descend. Nearing the bottom of its short descent the track heads left towards another metal farm gate. Here leave it, right, along a path – as indicated by a bridleway marker post – keeping the field boundary immediately alongside on the right.

Within a few yards the path reaches a wooden gate. Go through this into the corner of a field. Here follow the left-hand boundary. Nearing a field corner bear a few yards to the right to reach a metal farm gate through the boundary fence ahead, a pond just beyond. Pass through this gate and walk to the left of the pond, following the left-hand field boundary.

Where the boundary fence on the left ends, at an adjacent field corner, continue straight ahead – now following an incomplete boundary of hawthorn trees, again on the immediate left. Follow the line of hawthorns to the far side of the field and here ford a small stream and then pass through a metal farm gate into the next field. Here again follow the left boundary hedge, going straight ahead towards where

21

another metal farm gate will be seen – this sited about halfway along the field boundary. Pass through this gate into the next field. Here follow the right boundary fence, walking up a sunken path incompletely bordered by small trees/bushes on the left and the field boundary on the right. (*Note: This may be so overgrown as to necessitate leaving it to walk along its edge.*)

On reaching a wooden farm gate, across the sunken path, pass through this to proceed straight ahead along a dirt track. Follow the track out onto a quiet road – reached on a bend, with an isolated house ('Lower Ackhill') on the left (SO292656).

Turn right up the road. It climbs to a T-junction. Here go left – onto a quiet road leading to Ackhill House and Farm. When the road enters the farmyard, through a gate, bear right in front of the first outbuildings encountered. Rounding the far (right-hand) corner of these pass through another gate and bear left – between the outbuildings just rounded and another block (on the right). Walk between the buildings and pass through another metal gate, a metalled track now underfoot. Passing the end of the last of the outbuildings on the right, and with further outbuildings on the left, bear left at a Y-junction in the metalled track. The track begins to descend slightly towards more farm gates. Cross a cattle-grid at the farm gates and continue on the track, a large house immediately on the right.

The woodland up to the right here is Green Wood. Ahead, the higher hills of Radnor Forest are beginning to close in.

Follow the metalled track over another cattle-grid at more farm gates. Passing a few dwellings, right, it reaches a road – the B4356. Turn right along the road. It passes through the small settlement of Dolley Green.

Look out, on the right, for a small dwelling called 'Rose Villa' which is a joy to behold! It has a nicely carved wooden 'green man' head over its front door, two dragons outside it, a sun head over the right-hand window, a strange head over the left, and small owl/bird of prey heads of stone about its garden. Wonderful!

Ignore a road going left, at a junction between two chapel buildings, but continue along the B road. Ignore a track going up off the road, right.

The track to the right is the route of Offa's Dyke Path which now joins the Riversides Way for a short distance. It has made its way across the high ridge of hills, right, the nearest of which is Furrow Hill and the highest Hawthorn Hill.

Continue on the road for about another 220 yards after the junction with the track. Here (SO281655) leave it, left, to walk down a track and through a metal farm gate into a field. An Offa's Dyke Path sign points the way. ❷

Follow the left-hand boundary through the field to reach the River Lugg. *The small settlement visible across the river to the left is Discoed.*

Cross the river via a substantial metal footbridge (Dolley Old Bridge) and continue straight ahead along a riverside path. On reaching a sharp right bend in the river continue straight ahead, away from its bank for a few yards to locate an Offa's Dyke Path marker post under trees at the edge of a field, left. This indicates the main Offa's Dyke route plus another footpath and it is this latter which is now taken. From the riverbank and marker post bear half-right across the field.

Passing the corner of a field fence, immediately on the left, bear slightly left to round that corner and locate a stile in a fence ahead, situated just in from another fence corner. Cross this into the next field. Go straight ahead across the field from the stile to another stile in the boundary opposite. Cross this into the next field.

From the stile bear half-right to cross a footbridge over a sizeable stream, Cascob Brook. Over the footbridge, go straight ahead to another stile. Cross this, and immediately another, to enter the next field. Here follow the left-hand boundary.

Directly ahead now is Litton Hill which the route will shortly climb. To the right is Gilfach Wood, on the lower slopes of Furrow Hill. The hills leading up the right-hand side of the Lugg valley are visible half-right ahead, and include Gilfach Hill, Hengwm Hill and Cwm-Whitton Hill.

Follow the left-hand boundary through the field to reach a metal farm gate, just at the end of a small group of fir trees beyond the boundary on the left. Pass through this gate to enter another field. Go roughly straight ahead from the gate, following the natural contour along the bottom of the slope of the field, a boundary fence on the right initially about 15 yards away but this distance increasing as the field is crossed. Locate a stile in the far boundary and cross this into the next field.

Follow the left-hand boundary in the new field, climbing steadily. Just after passing under power lines, the left-hand boundary bears away to the left. Here continue straight ahead up the field, as indicated by a marker post alongside the corner in the boundary. Head towards the top right-hand corner of the field where a stile situated just to the left of a lone tree in the boundary gives access to a road – the B4357.

Turn right along the road. It soon passes a lone house on the left, a barn beyond it, and makes a bend to the right, starting to climb. Here, after about 240 yards in total on the road, turn left off it up a track (SO268663). (*Note: Two arms of this track leave the road, a small grassy triangle with bushes between them.*) ❸

Walk up the initially partly metalled track. After about 70 yards it loses its metalling and bends to the left. Here ignore a footpath which goes straight ahead through a gate and a track which goes off to the right past a barn.

Follow the obvious track as it bends left. It crosses a stream in a culvert and, about 35 yards after the marked left bend, reaches a Y-junction. Ignore the arm going left through metal farm gates towards a barn but instead take the right arm. The now dirt track immediately bends right and begins to climb. *This is the start of the climb up into Radnor Forest via Litton Hill. The steep track is bordered by masses of primroses in season.*

Continue up the steep, stony dirt track. It passes through a metal farm gate and then bends to the right before swinging left again. Ignore minor tracks and paths which join or leave it hereabouts but continue on the main, obvious route.

The track is joined by a field boundary on the left – a fence with hawthorn trees – and the rate of ascent lessens slightly, the track bending slightly to the right again. Since passing through the farm gate it has been in much wilder, open country.

About 100 yards before reaching a lone barn on the left of the track ignore two tracks which go off to the right – the one very sharply to the rear, the other (at a Y-junction) going down to cross a side valley on the right. Continue on the main track past the barn.

Passing the barn, the summit of Llan-fawr is half-right ahead. It rises to a height of 387 metres/1270 feet. As the climb up Litton Hill continues look behind to see the hills across the Lugg valley, previously mentioned.

The track continues to climb. The wire boundary fence on the left continues past the ruins of an old farmhouse – named as Upper House on Explorer Map 201 – before ending at a field corner. The track continues straight ahead beyond this but then begins to bear round to the right. Ignore a lesser track going off to the left here at a very indistinct Y-junction.

Although it is now less distinct than formerly the now grassier track is still fairly easy to follow. It bends towards the summit of Llan-fawr and becomes very wide. Keep to the right-hand side of it, ignoring another track which goes off to the left. With a pond ahead, the track swings sharply right to cross a small depression through which a stream is culverted, the aforementioned pond above and to the left.

Across the depression follow the now much less distinct grassy track straight ahead, a couple of fenced fields about 50 to 100 yards over to the right. This is another very wide section of indistinct grassy track. The distance between the track and the fields reduces as progress is made. On reaching a point opposite a metal farm gate in the corner of the nearer of the two fields bear half-left to climb a grassy slope ahead, the track still just about visible underfoot. The climb up the slope is quite steep. As it eases there is a 'crossroads' of tracks with that on the left climbing to the summit of Llan-fawr (technically NOT a right of way but a possible option here!). Go straight on here, the track underfoot becoming slightly more obvious again.

If climbing the slope up to the track 'crossroads' on a clear day look to the right for superb views down the Lugg valley and through the Presteigne Gap. Both Wapley and Shobdon Hills with their wooded 'upturned boat' shapes – familiar from Stage 1 of the Riversides Way – may be visible.

Another major track joins sharp right (SO255666). Continue straight ahead on the wider, obvious track formed by the coming together of the two. ❹

Look straight across the Lugg valley here to see the church (page 27) and battle site (page 28) at Pilleth, the latter marked by four large wellingtonia trees in the field above the church. Pilleth is mentioned in Domesday Book (1086) where it is referred to as 'Pelelei'. At this time it and the surrounding area, known as Maelienydd, were in the possession of the Mortimers of Wigmore, the powerful family of Marcher Earls.

Soon after the junction the track begins a gradual descent.

To the left a long high hill bearing a mast comes into view. This is Black Mixen, not quite the highest point in the Radnor Forest at 650 metres/2133 feet.

On reaching a metal gate (SO251668) pass through it to enter a field. Proceed along the right hand boundary of this, the descent soon becoming more marked. (Note: Just before reaching the gate a track from the summit of Llan-fawr joins the main track from the left.)

The wooded hill half right is Black Hill and the settlement at the far end of it, at the foot of its slope, is Monaughty – directly ahead as the sweeping left bend (below) begins. The River Lugg cuts through the hills here. The rounded hill beyond the village is Glog Hill.

Both grassy track and field boundary make a sweeping bend to the left descending to reach a junction ('crossroads') with a sunken track (SO245671).

On the sweeping bend down, nearing the 'crossing' of the sunken track, the settlement of Cascob appears directly ahead down in the valley of Cascob Brook.

On reaching the crossing of the sunken track turn left down it. The track immediately bends to the right and then left, below two large rocky outcrops on the right, and continues the steady descent. It passes through a farm gate. Continue straight ahead from this.

There are good views of the slopes of Llan-fawr over to the left from this point.

The track continues with farm buildings on its right and a stream (Cascob Brook, for the second time on this stage of the Riversides Way) on its left. It soon reaches a T-junction with a quiet road, just to the right of where the latter has crossed Cascob Brook via a sturdy bridge. Turn right along the road and at a junction go right. **❺**

Go left at the road junction if visiting Cascob church, dedicated to St. Michael (page 29). If the church is found to be locked try the cottage opposite for the key. There is a telephone box next to the entrance to the churchyard.

Continue along the road from the junction – a long, steep climb now starting on it. After about half a mile, as rate of climb lessens, at a road junction go right – a sign for Woodgate at the corner.

The hard work of the climb up the road out of Cascob is relieved, in season, by the profusion of wildflowers growing on the banks along it, violets being especially prolific here. Another good view of Llan-fawr to the right from the road up to Woodgate.

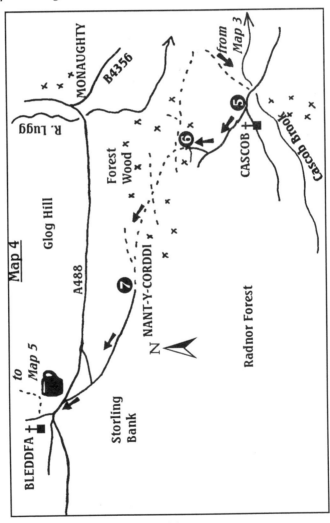

At the top of the climb up this short road the route passes what is marked on Explorer Map 201 as Woodgate Farm but appears to be more of a sawmill and timber yard. In its yard, at the time of writing, stood a large carved wooden bear. As we reached a point on the road level with the yard one May afternoon we were greeted by two goats which then proceeded to follow us into the forest until we were forced to stop and drive them back towards their exasperated owner!

The narrow road climbs from the junction. At a further junction ignore a metalled track going left but remain on the road to reach the timber yard at Woodgate Farm – on the left. Where the metalled road bends left into the timber yard leave it, continuing straight ahead through a wooden farm gate (may be open) into woodland (Forest Wood) on a dirt track (SO233671). **6**

Ignore a bridleway which goes right off the track immediately after the gate into the woods but continue down the main track. About 100 yards after the gate, at a 'crossroads' of forest tracks go straight ahead. The track descends and bears slightly to the left. The descent becomes steeper and the track drops down onto a much wider, major forest track. Go right along this for just a few yards and then sharp left off it down a narrower track again, maintaining the general direction taken through the woodland. The steady descent continues along a fairly straight section of track. Passing through a metal farm gate the woodland is left behind and the track becomes more sunken in nature.

Half-right ahead, up the valley, the buildings of Bleddfa make their first appearance.

Becoming more sunken and enclosed between its grassy banks the track approaches the small farming settlement of Nant-y-corddi. It

Pilleth Church

The church of St. Mary, Our Lady of Pilleth, is stunningly sited on the remote hillside with beautiful views over the Lugg Valley, a typical Celtic site. The church is very simple inside and out.

The oldest parts of the existing building date from a thirteenth century structure which was lengthened and had a tower added in the fourteenth century. The church was burnt by Owain Glyn Dwr in the early years of the fifteenth century but was later restored, including a new tower. The remains of the base of the older, and larger, tower can be seen to the north of the existing structure.

In 1894 another fire, caused by an overheating chimney, again gutted the church – only the tower surviving on this occasion. The church remained a burnt out shell until 1905 when Walter Tapper, then Surveyor of York Minster, was asked to restore the building. This restoration was completed in 1911 and included a 'temporary' roof which is obviously much lower than the original and today looks better suited for a garage than a church.

Sadly the condition and state of repair of the building is currently not all that could be hoped for. One of its walls leans alarmingly and is supported by a large wooden buttress outside while the 'temporary' roof is not quite managing to keep the worst of the weather out. From the inside holes around the margins of the roof become obvious and water and green stains disfigure some of the internal walls. A major restoration appeal was launched in 1999.

In the churchyard is a plain unmarked kerbstone marking the mass grave of some of the soldiers who died at the battle of Pilleth. Many bones dating from this time have been found in the churchyard – far more in fact than the size of the local population could account for – and these were buried on this particular spot in the mid nineteenth century.

About the same time more remains of the battle dead were buried on the hill above the church – known as Bryn Glas and thought likely to be the actual site of the main battle. Six Wellingtonia trees were planted to mark the spot and four of these remain to dominate the whole site.

The Battle of Pilleth

The battle took place on 22nd June 1402 between the Welsh under Owain Glyn Dwr and a larger English force under Sir Edmund Mortimer. Welsh victory was assured when the archers in Mortimer's army, mainly men of Welsh descent, went over to Glyn Dwr's side and turned their weapons against their erstwhile companions. It was a bloody battle with anything up to 1100 English dead and Sir Edmund Mortimer captured.

The savagery of the day did not end there, with the Welsh women camp followers then mutilating the corpses and demanding payment of ransom before burial would be allowed.

An interesting postscript to the battle is that the English King, Henry IV, delayed in sending the ransom demanded for the release of Mortimer – possibly because the Mortimers themselves had such a strong claim to the English throne – with the result that the latter himself made an alliance with Glyn Dwr, marrying one of his daughters (Catherine). This was followed, in 1405, by the Tripartite Indenture, an agreement formalised at Bangor whereby Glyn Dwr, the Mortimers and the Earls of Northumberland were to unite against the king and split the country three ways – with Glyn Dwr taking Wales and the Borders, Northumberland the country north of the River Trent, and Mortimer the south. It seems unlikely that Mortimer was ever directly involved in this alliance, which came to nothing, and the main architect of it was probably the Earl of Northumberland. Owain Glyn Dwr, Sir Edmund Mortimer and Harry Hotspur are depicted as involved in this plotting in Shakespeare's *Henry IV, Part 1*.

passes through a metal farm gate to reach a T-junction with another track. Turn left along this. It immediately passes through another metal farm gate (may be open) and bears around to the right, crossing a small stream via a bridge. Ignore an arm of the track going up to a dwelling on the left but go straight ahead, a slight rise, between two blocks of agricultural outbuildings. Passing through another metal farm gate, between the buildings, the track takes on a metalled surface to become a quiet road. ❼

The long grassy hill half-left along here is Storling Bank. The hill half-right ahead beyond Bleddfa is Pitch Hill – climbed on Stage 3 of the Riversides Way. The hill immediately to the right across the valley is Glog Hill. The route of the walk is here parallel to the course of the Elan Valley Aqueduct which runs,

St Michael's Church, Cascob

In the New Testament Book of Revelations Michael is mentioned as a fighter against dragons. There is a local legend that the last Welsh dragon lies asleep somewhere deep in Radnor Forest and that four churches were built long ago to surround the forest and were dedicated to St. Michael to make sure that the dragon does not escape and ravage the countryside. The legend has it that if any of the four churches is destroyed then this will in fact happen. The four churches are this one and those at Cefnllys, Llanfihangel Nant Melan and Llanfihangel Rhydithon.

St. Michael's church dates from the thirteenth century with a late fifteenth century tie-beam roof, which was restored in 1895. Inside, it consists of a nave and sanctuary. There is a fine oak screen, dating from the fourteenth century, dividing the two. An octagonal font dates from the same period. In the sanctuary is a rare sacring bell which traditionally was rung at funerals and dates from the fifteenth century. On the north wall of the nave is an 'abracadabra charm' dating from about 1700 and supposedly used to exorcise a young woman, Elizabeth Lloyd, from demon possession.

Outside, a collapsed west tower of the fourteenth century lies under a mound beside the current tower. The churchyard is circular in shape, which suggests a burial ground much older than the current building, possibly Celtic in origin.

The church was one of those locally which was burnt by Owain Glyn Dwr in the early years of the fifteenth century; possibly the reason for the collapsed tower.

There is some debate as to the origin of the name 'Cascob'. Some argue that it is a mutation of the Welsh words 'Cae' and 'Esgob' which would translate as 'the Bishop's Meadow'. This would seem to be unlikely however. *Domesday Book* (1086) has it as 'Cascope' which means 'the eminence/mound overlooking the Cas', the stream running nearby. This seems more likely.

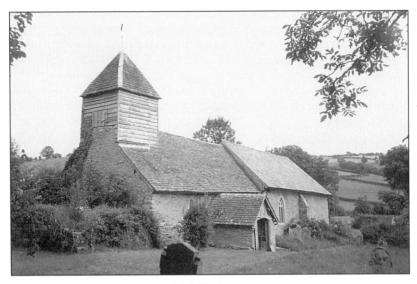

Bleddfa church

concealed, along the lower slopes of Glog Hill en route from mid Wales to Birmingham.

Follow the quiet road towards Bleddfa. *En route* it crosses a stream via a low bridge. At a road junction ignore a road going right but continue straight ahead. The narrow road eventually reaches a T-junction with the busy A488, just to the east of Bleddfa.

About 25 yards before the T-junction with the A488 wooden 'stiles' in the hedgerows on either side of the narrow road mark the crossing point (unseen) of the Elan Valley Aqueduct (See note at Stage 5).

Turn left up the A488, crossing as soon as it is safe to do so. Walk the short distance (under 300 yards) along it to reach the settlement of Bleddfa. This stage of the Riversides Way ends at the Hundred House Inn just across the triangular green on the right.

Bleddfa

Bleddfa lies on the A488 road, at a height of 700 feet above sea level. The name is pronounced 'Bleth-va', with the emphasis on the first syllable, and is an anglicised version of the Welsh name 'Bleidd fach' meaning 'the place of wolves', although whether this means where wolves were driven down from the forest and killed – in a wolf-pit – or merely refers to the large numbers of these animals hereabouts is uncertain. Wolves roamed wild in the Radnor Forest until Tudor times.

The village has the Bleddfa Centre (Gallery, Shop, Tea Room and Garden in old school buildings), the Hundred House Inn, a telephone

---

kiosk, a small Post Office, and the church of St. Mary Magdalene – an unusual dedication hereabouts, probably Norman replacing an earlier Celtic one – possibly founded as early as the sixth century.

The present church dates back to the early part of the thirteenth century, the nave remaining from this structure. In the late thirteenth century the building was extended to double its size and the junction can be clearly seen both inside and outside. The tower dated from much the same period but collapsed in medieval times, also destroying much of the west end of the nave. Parts of the remains of this can be seen outside at the west end of the building. Recent excavations of these ruins have revealed the cause of its demise to be burning which gives credence to the story that this is another of the churches locally which was burnt by Owain Glyn Dwr in the early years of the fifteenth century – just like Cascob, passed earlier on this stage of the walk.

Inside the church, the octagonal font is medieval. The roof dates from the fifteenth/sixteenth centuries. Many of the internal roof timbers would have been painted and the rood beam still retains some floral decoration – red on a white background – with traces on others. The wooden bell turret at the west end of the stone roof was built in 1711.

There are the remains of a motte and bailey fortification to the east of the village. Dating from the twelfth century it was not rebuilt after Llywelyn ap Gruffyd destroyed it in 1262. Otherwise the only other building of any great age is the Hundred House Inn. Earliest reference to a building on this site dates from 1527. Courts of the Hundred were held at Bleddfa from 1524 onwards and continued to be held in the present building until 1867 when they were moved to Penybont.

The Riversides Way Clun Extension

A two day extension to the Riversides Way - from Knighton to Clun and return - is in preparation and is designed either to be undertaken as a separate walk or included within the main walk, increasing it to ten stages.

The new walk includes a section of Offa's Dyke *en route* to Clun while the return journey takes in the impressive Rock of Woolbury - a quarry used in the construction of Clun castle. Later, it samples the delights of the beautiful and largely unknown Redlake valley, with superb views of Caer Caradoc hill fort therein, before crossing Stow Hill and visiting Stowe church, high on its slopes and with superb views across the Teme valley. Details/guide available from David Milton early in 2002. Contact him on 0121 742 1231.

Stage 3

Bleddfa to Knighton

Mileage: 7½ Miles; (From Bleddfa: 2¼ miles to Llangynllo)
O.S.Maps: 1:50000 (Landranger): 137 (Ludlow);
1:25000 (Explorer): 201 (Knighton & Presteigne)

Using tracks and fieldpaths, the route climbs north out of Bleddfa, via Pitch Hill, to reach the Lugg valley and visit the sleepy little village of Llangynllo (Llangunllo) – and its dragon.

Another climb – paths and a quiet road – take it eastwards over Bailey Hill, with superb views over both Lugg and Teme valleys en route. A long descent towards Knighton – over tracks – ends with a walk along the lower slopes of Garth Hill to enter the town.

STARTING outside the Hundred House Inn, facing the small triangular green, turn right – (i.e. away from the A488) – along the road, past the sub-post office. After about 50 yards leave the road, right, for a track which descends, passing through a gateway, to reach a stream. Cross this via a simple but sturdy footbridge alongside a ford.

Over the stream go straight ahead to pass through a metal farm gate. Bear half-left to follow an obvious track through the field so entered. After not too many yards this bears right and begins to climb. *This is the start of the climb up Pitch Hill.*

Nearing the corner of woodland – just beyond the field boundary on the right – the by now less distinct track swings left up the hill. Remain on it. As a rough guide follow the bottom edge of a large grouping of gorse bushes – on the right. The steep climb continues.

Behind, views back across to the northern hills of Radnor Forest are already beginning to open up, with the lower Storling Bank in the foreground.

As it skirts the gorse bushes the track underfoot becomes more distinct again. It approaches a boundary hedge on the left – hawthorn bushes/trees – and climbs alongside this. Ignore a gap at a corner of the hedge alongside but continue to climb straight ahead up the hill on the obvious track. *There is a good view behind back down on Bleddfa and its church from this point.*

Where the track again becomes indistinct continue almost straight ahead, bearing very gradually towards the boundary on the left – an incomplete boundary of trees – and eventually walking alongside this. Nearing a boundary fence ahead bear half-right to pass through a metal farm gate in this. It leads into what seems to be a livestock impounding

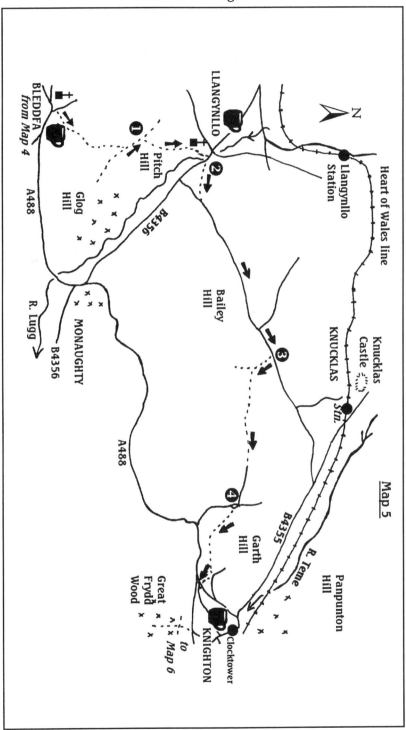

area, surrounded by fences. Go straight ahead through this from the gate, an intermediate boundary fence on the immediate left, to a stile in the facing fence. Cross this into the next field.

Go straight ahead from the stile to reach a metal farm gate in the next boundary, the climb now easing. A stony farm track is met just before the gate. Having passed through the gate DO NOT follow the stony track but instead parallel its course as it bears half-left walking some yards to its right and above it, an old an incomplete single strand of wire fence between. (The stony track leads to a small disused quarry – at SO212690). Aim for a metal farm gate through the fence over to the left.

Passing through the farm gate go almost straight ahead, just very slightly right, to skirt the highest ground on the hill – which is just to the right. Walk towards a farm gate in the boundary fence ahead and pass through this.

NOTE: AT THE TIME OF WRITING, NEARLY ALL OF THE MANY FARM GATES BETWEEN BLEDDFA AND LLANGYNLLO BEAR YELLOW MARKER TAPE TO SHOW THE ROUTE OF THE RIGHT OF WAY.

The walk here is at a height of about 365 metres/ 1197 feet. Another good view down to the left of Bleddfa church and village from this gate.

Bear half-right from the gate to cross higher ground in the new field. Aim to keep a group of pine trees on a hill opposite slightly to the left, and a distant isolated farm (Tre-boeth) directly to the left, as progress is made. Head for a field corner where there is a metal farm gate (SO211697).

Passing through the gate immediately turn left through another gateway – (gate may be open) – to enter another field. Follow the left-hand boundary through this – a wire fence with hawthorn hedge behind it.

On reaching the end of the field pass through a metal farm gate. In the next field continue to follow the left-hand boundary for about 45 yards but then, as it bears slightly left towards a metal farm gate ahead, go half-right – away from it – to parallel the boundary fence which was ahead but is now to the left (SO210699). (Note: The farm gate seen ahead as the turning is made does bear yellow marker tape but this marks the course of another right of way and not the one now taken.) ❶

Continue with the boundary fence parallel on the left, and about 45 yards distant, until reaching another fence ahead. Bear left along this to pass through it via a metal farm gate at the field corner.

The Lugg valley comes into view ahead. The large hill half-right across it is Bailey Hill, crossed later on this stage of the Riversides Way.

Go straight ahead from the gate down the next field, the boundary to the left bending slightly away. Maintain direction to drop down steeply and rejoin the left boundary fence as it bends back again. Locate and pass through a metal farm gate in that boundary, situated just where a rough dirt track begins alongside it. A stream in a culvert is crossed immediately before the gate.

Through the gate, go straight ahead following an obvious depression/contour in the land, a sunken track developing as the field is crossed – although this may be so overgrown as to necessitate leaving it to walk along its edge. On reaching a metal farm gate pass through this to enter the next field. Here bear half-right, again following the natural contour/indistinct track. This bends slightly to the left, a double wire field fence accompanying it on the right. Follow the fence along to the far corner of the field.

Look right here for superb views down the upper Lugg valley. Looking down the valley, the large hill on the right – the continuation of the hill (Pitch Hill) the route is now on is Glog Hill, which rises to a height of 408 metres/1338 feet.

Pass through a metal farm gate in the far corner of the field. Walk just a few yards along the right-hand boundary fence in the next field and then pass through a metal farm gate into the adjacent field on the right. Through the gate, turn left to descend this field alongside its left-hand boundary.

The woodland ahead is Great Wood. Llangynllo is hidden beyond it.

Walk down the length of this field alongside the left boundary – ignoring a metal farm gate through that boundary where it bends to the right – a fairly steep descent especially in its lower stages. On reaching the bottom left-hand corner of the field pass through a metal farm gate there – (may be open). Cross a stream in a dip beyond and climb the short bank up into the field ahead to reach an obvious farm track. Turn right down this.

Follow the farm track down the field, crossing a culverted stream *en route*. On drawing level with a metal farm gate through the boundary on the right, and at the near end of a row of small trees, leave the farm track, right, to reach the boundary fence and then continue down the field walking along a grassy 'avenue' between the boundary fence – on the right – and the row of trees – on the left.

At the end of the grassy 'avenue'/row of trees bear left to rejoin the farm track. After about 30 yards, as the track begins to bend to the left, towards farm buildings, drop down to the right off it to pass through a metal farm gate into a field – (may be open). Entering the field turn left to follow the left-hand boundary through it. On reaching a metal farm gate in the far corner of the field pass through this and again follow the left-hand boundary through the next field, farm buildings beyond that boundary on the left. At the far left-hand corner of the field pass through a metal farm gate onto a short length of track which leads out onto a quiet road – the B4356 – with the small village of Llangynllo (Llangunllo) just to the left. **❷**

On reaching the last gate before the road look over the right shoulder, behind, down the Lugg valley. The large wooded hill which dominates the view is Glog Hill again.

Turn right along the road to continue the walk or left to visit the village (see box on page 37).

 Llangynllo is linked to both Knighton and Bleddfa via a limited bus service operated by Owens Motors. Bus stop is by the war memorial, opposite the Greyhound pub and shop.

 Llangynllo also has a station on the Heart of Wales Railway Line but this is 1¼ miles distant from the village along the minor road which goes right at the crossroads by the war memorial.

Walk along the B4356 – here a very quiet road. It soon crosses the River Lugg. After about 220 yards in total on the road, just before reaching a row of dwellings on the left – 'Lugg View' – leave the road, left, onto initially a metalled drive to a house. When, after just a few yards, this bends left to the dwelling leave it, right, to climb up a narrow path behind the 'Lugg View' properties (SO215712).

The narrow path is initially bounded by a hedgerow, on the left, and a high fir hedge, on the right. Where the latter ends it is replaced by

Topiary dragon in Llangynllo

Llangynllo

Llangynllo (Llangunllo) – 'the church of St Cynllo' – is a sleepy little village nestling in the upper Lugg valley. Entering it from the direction of the walk a lane going off to the left leads directly up to the churchyard, but this can also be visited using a much more interesting route.

Continue through the village on the main street – the B4356. On the left a house sports a collection of old enamelled advertising signs. Quite a nostalgia trip for some of us! Further on is the war memorial and a combined pub and community shop – 'The Greyhound'. Turn left up the hill here to visit the church. Just a few steps past the shop/pub one is brought to a sudden halt by the sight of a Dragon! Fortunately it is of the topiary variety but one can only wonder at the skill and care that must be embellished on it.

At the top of a short climb turn left, in front of the old school buildings, to visit the church. The corner of the tower of the church bears a foundation stone dated 1896 but parts of the building are much older than this.

The church is dedicated to St Cynllo, a fifth or sixth century Celtic saint who was active in this area – other locations with similarly dedicated churches in this part of Wales include Llanbister, Nantmel and Rhayader. Records show the existence of a church here since Norman times but the earliest part of the building seen today is a lancet window in the north wall which dates from the thirteenth century. The adjoining double arch which now forms the entrance to the vestry is fifteenth century and probably part of an earlier building on the site. In the window ledge of the vestry is a stone dated 1687 which is said to have been taken from the south wall of the original tower. The present tower actually dates from 1894, not 1896 as per the foundation stone.

At the back of the church, near the font, is an early school desk from the National School, Llangynllo, which was opened in 1863 and closed in 1984, the premises passed *en route* to the church. The earliest record of a school in the village however dates from 1653.

garden boundary fences. Cross a stile to the left of a wooden gate to enter a field. Follow the left-hand boundary up this, a steep climb now underway.

Look behind for views over to Pitch Hill and the route used to descend into Llangynllo earlier.

At the top of the field pass through a metal farm gate in the boundary. Go straight ahead up the next field towards a stile which will be seen in its top boundary. On reaching this cross it and go straight across a stony track which runs along above that boundary fence. Still climbing steeply, continue straight ahead up the new field, gradually approaching a stand of conifers which will be seen to the right above.

Nearing the conifers, head towards a marker post which is situated just under the edge of the trees. Pass to the right of the post and follow an obvious sunken path upwards, another marker post further up the path confirming the route. Bear to the right of this post to continue climbing to a stile. Cross the stile onto a quiet road.

Look behind from the stile for views across as far as Pool Hill (506 metres/1660 feet), on the slopes of which the River Lugg rises, and its neighbours.

Turn left along the road. A lengthy (just under two miles) high-level walk along this now commences.

A few yards along the road turn and look back for superb views across to Pitch and Glog Hills and beyond to the Radnor Forest, with – slightly over to the left – the long mass of Black Mixen (650 metres/2133 feet), with its mast.

Walking along the road there are superb views to be had down to the right (east) – over the Lugg valley and beyond.

An initial section of road winds slightly and passes an isolated dwelling on the left – 'Cloggie' on Explorer Map 201. A fairly straight section follows, ending by passing the entrance drive to Coed-harbour – on the right. A general fairly gentle ascent continues.

The quiet, narrow road winds a little before another fairly straight section. Passing an isolated dwelling and then a small stand of conifers, on the right, and a corrugated metal outbuilding, on the left, the road bends left.

The road climbs along the main ridge of Bailey Hill which rises to a height of 426 metres/1398 feet at its highest point, just to the right here. The route along it here reaches a height of about 390 metres/1280 feet. Ahead, the hills across the Teme valley now appear.

Passing a second group of conifers, on the right, the road begins a slight descent and reaches a junction. Here ignore the road going left but continue straight ahead, soon passing the drive to Upper Dolwilkin, on the left.

Just beyond where the road passes a group of conifers, on the left of the road just after the entrance drive to Upper Dolwilkin, look left down into the Teme valley to see Knucklas Viaduct on the Heart of Wales railway line with the hilltop site of Knucklas Castle beyond it. A little further along the road more of the settlement of Knucklas itself comes into view while the best view of the viaduct, castle hill and village is gained just before turning off the road onto the track (see below).

The prominent hill almost straight ahead across the Teme valley is Cwm-sanaham Hill (406 metres/1332 feet).

Bleddfa to Knighton

About a quarter of a mile after the road junction leave the road, right, for a stony track – accessed through a metal farm gate. A footpath signpost points the way (SO245727). ❸

The track climbs slightly from the road. After about 300 yards – where the track starts to bend right, and with the corner of a field boundary hedge on the left – leave it, left, to walk down a less distinct track alongside the boundary hedge of the aforementioned field (on the right). A footpath sign again points the way, although it also shows the main track ahead as another public right of way. (Navigation Note: Leaving the main track there should be a line of pine trees on the top of a ridge straight ahead.)

Follow the rutted, grassy track alongside the field boundary hedge on the right. It drops down into a small stream valley, named on

Knucklas

The name 'Knucklas' is an anglicised version of the Welsh name for the settlement, which is Cnwc-las, meaning 'Green Mound' – presumably referring to the castle/hill fort site.

The scant ruins on the green hilltop site are thought to belong to a castle built here sometime between 1220 and 1230 by Hugh Mortimer and destroyed in 1262 by Llywelyn ap Gruffyd and again, in 1402, by Owain Glyn Dwr. This structure seems to have been built on the site of an earlier hill fort or castle which has Arthurian connections. Legend has it that the original castle here was the birthplace of King Arthur's queen, Guinevere. It is said that Arthur married Guinevere (Gwynhwyfar) at Cnwc-las and that the couple lived in the castle, founding the Round Table and mounting campaigns against the Saxon invaders. These claims are based on ancient Welsh legends – as told in the ballads and stories of the Mabinogion – which predate the Arthurian tales of Chretien de Troyes and Geoffrey of Monmouth. Given this, it would seem that Knucklas has as least as strong a claim to being considered as the site of Camelot as do Tintagel or Winchester.

Another story – connected with the site – is that stone from the ruins of the later castle was used in the construction of the railway viaduct alongside (Heart of Wales Line).

The thirteen arch viaduct was built in 1863 for the London & North-Western Railway. Designed by the German, H. Lotte, it is 190 yards long and rises to a maximum height of 75 feet above the valley of the Ffrwdwen Brook, a tributary of the River Teme. At either end of the structure are crenellated half-round corbelled turrets – which seem quite fitting given both its location and also the supposed source of some of its building stone. Another story concerning the viaduct is that of a fox which was being pursued by hounds across it and which leapt from it to its death.

Explorer Map 201 as 'Downes's Dingle', following the field boundary around to the right to a wooden farm gate and crossing a stream, in a culvert, just before reaching this. Pass through the gate to follow the still distinct grassy track up alongside the left-hand boundary (wire fence and scattered hawthorns), of the next field, the aforementioned line of trees on the ridge at the top of this – a steady climb.

On reaching the ridge-top pines, at the top of the field, the route attains a height of 392 metres/1286 feet. At the metal farm gate here pause to admire the superb views. Over to the right, behind, Black Mixen (650 metres/2133 feet), still dominates the horizon. Directly to the right is the flattened conical shape of Llan-fawr (387 metres/1270 feet) skirted on the climb up into Radnor Forest on Stage 2 of the Riversides Way. Slightly to the right, ahead in the distance, may be seen the buildings of Powys Observatory on top of Llan-wen Hill (417 metres/1368 feet) – passed on Stage 4 of the walk.

At the top of the field pass through a metal farm gate onto what is a much more significant stony dirt track – the ridge-top stand of pines just to the right (SO254723). The track immediately begins to descend slightly.

Walking down the track, stunning views open up ahead and to the left – down the Teme valley. Visible are Panpunton Hill (375 metres/1230 feet), above Knighton, and the hills on both sides of the Teme beyond – Stow Hill, Bucknell Wood and Bucknell Hill on the left of the valley; Ffridd and Llan-wen Hill (with observatory), on its right. It is the latter two which are crossed on the first part of Stage 4 of the walk. In the foreground, slightly to the left, the lower hill with the mast is Garth Hill (346 metres/1135 feet), around the lower slopes to the right of which this stage of the walk enters Knighton.

As the descent becomes steeper the outskirts of Knighton appear from behind the right side of Garth Hill. The woodland behind Knighton is Great Frydd Wood, on the lower slopes of Ffridd. Above the wood is Knighton golf course, while the earthworks of Offa's Dyke run along across the ridge of the hill.

Continue down the stony track, the descent becoming steeper. Passing the entrance drive to Ebrandy House, on the left, the track becomes metalled. The descent steepens again.

Garth Hill, with its mast, is now directly ahead.

In its lower stages the descent on the metalled track becomes very steep and 'sunken' between high banks.

The banks of the track are a riot of bluebells, celandines, violets and other wildflowers in season.

Passing a farm on the left – Little Cwm-gilla – the track bends right and finally reaches a road. At the junction go right, a stream channelled alongside on the right and a parallel short stretch of quiet road just over the hedge on the left. In about 50 yards, where this hedge ends, turn sharp left to walk back about 10 yards on the road on the other side of it and then leave this, right, to climb up a bank to a stile (SO268726). ❹

Cross the stile and follow the path straight ahead from it, climbing slightly. After a short distance a field boundary fence joins from the right. Follow the obvious path as it contours around the lower slopes of Garth Hill, the field boundary on its immediate right and footpath marker posts indicating the way. Well-used by livestock the path can be very muddy, while in late summer it can get overgrown with bracken and other vegetation. It crosses several springs *en route* which, again, can make it wet underfoot in places.

Continue to follow the field boundary on the right. Just after passing two metal farm gates through that boundary the path reaches a stile. Cross this into the field ahead. Here again follow the right-hand boundary hedge.

Where the right-hand field boundary turns away downhill to the right continue straight ahead towards a section of path which passes between hawthorn trees, following an obvious contour across the field. Passing between these trees drop down onto a more substantial stony track to maintain direction, farm outbuildings just to the right.

The outskirts of Knighton are now visible again half-right ahead.

Follow the obvious track. At a Y-junction in it take the right (lower) arm.

Look across the valley to the immediate right for a sighting of the Elan Valley Aqueduct crossing a side valley, opposite, via a substantial low pipeline bridge – on its 73 mile journey from mid Wales to Birmingham. See note at Stage 5 of the Riversides Way.

At another, less distinct, Y-junction follow the less distinct right arm towards a tree and the protruding corner of an adjacent field – almost straight ahead. (The clearer left arm climbs up the hill for a few yards and then bends back on itself.) Passing the field corner and tree (right) the track – which bears traces of tarmac in places – reaches a metal farm gate with a stile to its right. Cross the stile into the next field. Here follow the right-hand boundary, dropping down to a stile in its far right-hand corner.

Cross the stile to gain access to a road and turn right down this. After only about 15 yards, where the road bends left, leave it – going straight ahead at the bend – over a stile and down a very narrow footpath ahead. The path is bounded by a field boundary on the right and garden boundaries on the left. It descends steeply to reach a road, a final slope down to the left onto the pavement of this. Cross the road, bearing very slightly left, to reach another footpath opposite. This is accessed either over or around a stile.

The Riversides Way

The path is bounded by gardens on both sides. It runs straight across the end of a cul-de-sac to continue along another narrow section. Over a stile and down some steps, the path emerges onto a quiet road. Turn left along this. After 20 yards leave the road, right, along a narrow road/wide path which is marked as being 'Unsuitable for Motor Vehicles'. The wide metalled path drops down to join a stream, on the right, the two running alongside each other for some distance.

When the path widens and leaves the stream continue on it – straight ahead. Ignore a path going up to the left. Remain on what is now a road, the stream again visible down to the right but then finally bending away out of sight. Ignore another path going left.

Ignore a turning right – George Close – but continue to follow the road to emerge onto Broad Street in the centre of Knighton, the George & Dragon pub on the left corner at the junction. Turn left to reach the clock tower where this stage of the Riversides Way ends.

Knighton

Knighton literally means 'the town/settlement of the knights'. However its Welsh name, Tref-y-clawdd, is more significant meaning 'The Town on the Dyke' which emphasises the importance of its position astride that fortification built under King Offa of Mercia around AD780. The crossing point on the River Teme here must have also contributed to the early growth of the settlement while in more recent times the arrival of the railway, in the 1860s, brought a degree of prosperity. Latterly the town has seen a growth in tourism due in no small part to its central position on the Offa's Dyke National Trail. The Offa's Dyke Centre is situated in the town.

The town was given the name of Tref-y-clawdd in about AD840 by the Welsh king Rhodri Mawr (Roderick the Great). It is in *Domesday Book* (1086) that it is called Chenistetone – the town of the retainers or armed freemen (later knights). After that it was variously referred to as Chnicheton, Kenithtun or Knyteton – by Saxon, Welshman or Norman.

The middle of the town – Broad Street – is marked by a fine clock tower of 1872, quite a common feature in Welsh towns. Off Broad Street by the clock tower is High Street, also known as the Narrows, which dates from Tudor times but today contains buildings mainly from the seventeenth century. One side of this street was called the 'Salutation Inn', the houses being dovetailed into each other suggesting they were once part of a single building.

Near the top of High Street, in a private garden, are the scant remains of Knighton Castle. Probably founded in the eleventh century it was partially destroyed, in 1215, by Llywelyn ap Iorwerth. By 1230 it was under the control of the Mortimers and in 1262 was destroyed by Llywelyn ap Gruffyd. Restored by the Mortimers it was finally destroyed by Owain Glyn Dwr in 1402

Set back from the street where the Narrows joins Broad Street is the Old House. Its seventeenth century half-timbered front hides a medieval cruck built structure – formerly an open hall. Smoke-blackened roof timbers herein indicate the earlier existence of an open fire on a central hearth with no chimney but just a smoke hole in the roof above.

The other significant building in the town is the Church of St. Edward – situated in Church Road. There was previously an eleventh century church on this site, itself replacing an older building, but this was largely demolished in 1756 and all that now remains of it is the lower tower. The new church of 1756 has itself been replaced by the current Victorian building although the top of the tower is a survivor from it. The Victorian building was built in two stages – the nave in 1876 and the chancel 20 years later.

The dedication of the present church is to Edward the Confessor, King of England, who died in 1066. If it seems unusual for a Welsh church to be dedicated to an English king/saint then it must be remembered that until the establishment of the Church in Wales, in the 1920s, Knighton was in the diocese of Hereford.

When the eighteenth century church was taken down, in 1876, the oak from the box pews was reused as panelling in the lounge bar of the George & Dragon public house, in Broad Street, which itself dates from 1637. A good excuse to visit this pub!

A Town Trail to Knighton can be obtained from the Offa's Dyke Centre/Tourist Information Office.

Knighton and the Clock Tower

Stage 4

Knighton to Lingen

Mileage: 9 Miles (From Knighton: 4 miles to Powys Observatory;
6 miles to Willey Chapel)
Maps: 1:50000 (Landranger): 137 (Ludlow);
1:25000 (Explorer): 201 (Knighton & Presteigne)

The route shares that of Offa's Dyke Path as it climbs out of Knighton, via footpath and road walking. After about two miles in the company of the national trail it goes its own way, making a high level crossing of Llan-wen Hill, on a good track, and passing Powys Observatory. There are superb views to be had along this section.

After a section of high road the route enters England and, still on roads, descends as it heads east. The stage ends with a climb over Harley's Mountain, via tracks and footpaths, before descending to the quiet settlement of Lingen. There are more wonderful panoramic views from the top of Harley's Mountain.

STARTING at the clock tower walk down Broad Street and turn right through the arch of the Knighton Hotel and across the car park beyond. Continuing straight ahead climb up a steep road (Larkey Lane) to reach a T-junction.

Look behind here for good views across Knighton to Kinsley Wood beyond. The letters 'ER', formed by the planting of a different species of trees within a dark green coniferous stand in the wood may be seen. This commemorates the coronation of Queen Elizabeth II and these trees will not be felled until after her death. The effect is best appreciated in the spring or autumn.

Turn right and then immediately left off the road up Frydd Terrace, between the houses, as indicated by an Offa's Dyke sign. At the rear of the houses turn right, in front of a row of garages. Passing the end of these walk a few yards up the entrance drive to a house and then turn half left up a steep footpath which leads over a stile into woodland. On reaching a metalled track cross straight over it, a concrete Offa's Dyke Path marker a few yards up the path which continues the steep climb through the trees – Great Frydd Wood. At the top of the wood cross its upper boundary fence, over a stile, and turn right to follow it along, Knighton Golf Course on the left. Initially still climbing, the path soon levels out, still following the boundary of the wood – to the right.

The climb out of Knighton is up Ffridd Hill and the height here about 320 metres/1050 feet. As the trees to the right thin out there are good views of Garth Hill, topped by a mast, slightly to the rear.

44

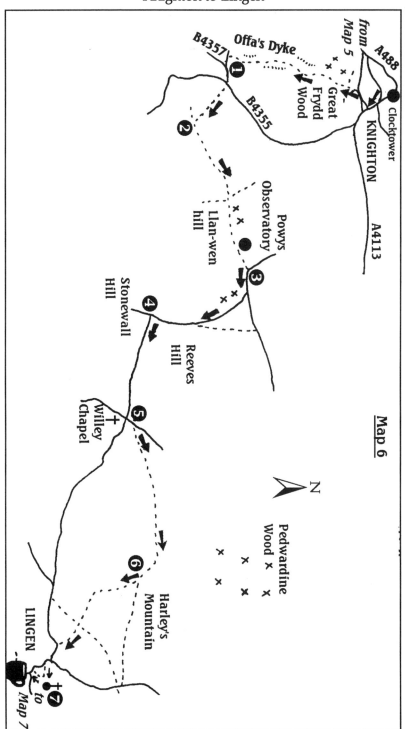

Cross a stile, to the right of a metal gate, to enter a field and leave the Golf Course behind. Follow the right hand boundary of the field, the woodland on the right now thinning out. Continue to follow the right hand boundary through three further fields, each one entered over a stile.

Notice on the upright of all the stiles the little representation of an Offa coin, the symbol of the Offa's Dyke Association, although the waymarking throughout is with the National Trail 'acorn'.

The Dyke itself has been on the right of the path since it emerged from the woods but has been, until now, fairly insignificant in size. It is shortly to be crossed and thereafter becomes much more pronounced. The prominent hill visible on the left along here with the Powys Observatory building at its summit is Llan-wen Hill – 'the hill of sunshine'. It is 417 metres/1368 feet in height and is crossed by the route of the Riverside Way later on this stage.

Follow the path along the right hand boundary of the third field, with the bank of Offa's Dyke to the right. On reaching a gap through the earthwork (at SO280708) cross it and continue to a stile over the right hand boundary fence. Cross this and turn left to follow the boundary through the field so entered, the Dyke just beyond it and becoming more prominent.

Continue to follow the left hand boundary fence through two more fields, both entered over stiles. On reaching the far boundary of the second of these cross a stile which is situated midway between the Dyke on the left and the field boundary on the right, where the field narrows. Go straight across the field so entered to a stile opposite. Cross this and again go straight across the next field to another stile opposite. Cross this and again initially go straight ahead, to eventually follow the right hand field boundary to another stile. Cross this and continue to follow the right hand boundary, the Dyke immediately on the right. On reaching a stile in the right hand boundary cross it onto a road. **❶**

On the field side of this stile is carved 'Chepstow 78 Miles' and on the road side 'Prestatyn 98 Miles'.

Crossing the stile onto the road look straight ahead for a view of the flattened conical shaped hill of Llan-fawr (387 metres/1270 feet) at the north-eastern corner of Radnor Forest – skirted on Stage 2. Half right the long high hill bearing a mast is Black Mixen (650 metres/2133 feet). To its left is Bache Hill, 610 metres/2001 feet high.

Turn left along the road. At a road junction, after about 50 yards, go left. An Offa's Dyke sign indicates the way. There is a telephone box on the left at the junction. When the road makes a T-junction with the B4355 road (at SO282697) go straight across that road and up a track opposite. (Offa's Dyke Path goes right here, along the B4355.) The

---

Offa's Dyke

Offa's Dyke takes its name from Offa II of Mercia, the first Saxon leader to bear the title 'King of the English'. He ruled between AD757 and 796.

The dyke was constructed sometime after AD780 to mark and fortify the western boundary of his kingdom and was probably the result of an agreement between Offa and the Welsh, or Cymr. There appear to have been jointly administered laws governing trade and movement across the dyke and the recovery of stolen livestock. It was therefore almost as much a trade boundary as a defensive structure.

---

straight dirt/grassy track climbs steadily. At a track 'crossroads' go straight on.

There are good views across the Teme valley to the hills beyond on the left as the track climbs. Stow Hill is particularly prominent. It rises to something over 430 metres/1410 feet. Powys Observatory is half-left.

About half a mile after leaving the road the track makes a T-junction with another track, marked as Llan-wen Hill on Ordnance Survey maps. Here turn left onto a wide grassy track which continues the steady climb. ❷

Within 100 yards on the track superb views open up on both sides. Presteigne may be seen far to the right, in the Lugg valley, with Wapley Hill to the left beyond it. To the left of the track the hills across the Teme valley still dominate. Stowe church is visible in the folds of Stow Hill. Passing the first of two conifer plantations on the right of the track look left for a view of Knighton below, its church prominent.

Continue on the track, passing two small plantations of conifers which are to the right. The track continues to climb. After almost a mile on the track, at a slightly staggered track 'crossroads' go straight on (SO301699). The track passes through a metal farm gate to follow the left hand boundary of a field, a conifer plantation beyond that boundary.

On a clear day turn around at the gate and look behind for a good view of Black Mixen, the long hill with the mast, in Radnor Forest. Entering the field look right, over the top of the conifers, for a superb view of Knighton, the whole town now visible in the valley below. Garth Hill can be seen above the town to the left and most of the route of this stage to date can be made out. Powys Observatory building is half-left ahead.

Straight ahead views to the east begin to open up with Titterstone Clee Hill in the far distance and the twin ridges of Mortimer Forest in front of it. To the right of these the long wooded hill is Gatley Long Coppice. The hills across the Teme valley are soon visible as far around as those above and beyond the settlement of Bucknell – Bucknell Wood, Bucknell Hill and Hopton Titterhill.

Pass through a gateway out of the field. The track passes the entrance drive to the observatory building – on the left – and at last begins to descend, soon reaching a road. ❸

Powys Observatory is situated at a height of about 417 metres/1368 feet on Llan-wen Hill. It was built in 1995. The main dome of the building houses the telescopes, the largest of which is a 13 inch refractor. A camera obscura, planetarium, weather station, and seismology section are also on site. Unfortunately the privately owned building is not, at the time of writing, open to the public. On the left of the drive to the observatory there is a stone circle. This was built in 1997 and is dedicated to the late Diana, Princess of Wales (1961-1997).

Turn right along the road.

Not many yards along the road look left for the best view yet of Stowe Church nestling among the folds of Stow Hill, on the opposite side of the Teme valley.

At a road junction turn right. This road is initially bordered by coniferous plantations on its right. It climbs and bends slightly right before straightening out and gently undulating.

Once the conifer plantations bordering the road have been left behind there are good views to the right of Black Mixen and the top of the conical Whimble, both in Radnor Forest. The Whimble rises to 599 metres/1965 feet. The Clee Hills are still visible over to the left. On reaching the top of the climb on the road look behind left for a good view of the observatory on Llan-wen hill. The northern escarpment of the Black Mountains is visible ahead.

As the road makes a long bend to the right, after a little over half a mile on it, ignore a bridleway going off sharply to the left (SO318694). The road is by now fairly level.

From a point just before where the bridleway leaves the road until the next road junction the road marks the boundary between Wales (Powys) and England (Herefordshire). The latter is entered as the left turning is taken at the junction.

At a road junction turn left. ❹

At the turning look left for good views across Mortimer Forest to Titterstone Clee Hill beyond. The latter rises to a height of 533 metres/1748 feet.

The road descends, gradually at first but then more steeply.

Half-left ahead is the round mass of Harley's Mountain, with its mix of large arable and pastoral fields. It rises to a height of 386 metres/1266 feet and takes its name from the Harley family who resided, and still do to this day, at nearby Brampton Bryan and had rights over much of the land hereabouts. Most of the remainder of this stage of the walk is spent crossing it.

The long flat topped and wooded hill straight ahead is Shobdon Hill Wood (319 metres/1046 feet), while the similarly shaped hill half-right is Wapley Hill (329 metres/1079 feet), which has an Iron Age hill fort at its summit covering 25 acres, one of several hill forts in this area which have been suggested as the site of the last stand of Caractacus against the Romans. Both are old friends from Stage 1. The more rounded wooded hill in the foreground between the two is Cole's Hill. The River Lugg flows between it and its two neighbours.

The road descends to a staggered crossroads. Here go left, signposted 'Leintwardine'. **❺**

Not many yards along the road straight ahead at the crossroads is Willey Chapel. There are two buildings here – the original Willey chapel of 1869, built in brick, and a smaller building which used to be the chapel at Hergest but was dismantled and moved here in 1937. The chapel closed in 1985 due to falling attendance and is now a private residence.

About 150 yards along the road, just as it starts to descend, leave it for a bridleway which goes off to the right (SO332686) through a metal farm gate and into a field . Walk up the grassy track, bordered on the right by trees – a mixture of hazels, hawthorns and rowans.

A few yards up the grassy track look left for unexpected views as far as the Long Mynd and its outlier, Caer Caradoc, which lie on either side of Church Stretton (not visible). The prominent part wooded hill in the foreground is Pedwardine Wood, behind which is the Park and settlement of Brampton Bryan. The climb now starting is that over Harley's Mountain. Walking here in August we saw a large number of dragonflies.

Climb up the track to reach another metal farm gate. Pass through this into the next field, the track now bordered on both sides by trees, a wire fence also on the left. Still climbing, the track reaches another metal farm gate. Again pass through this and remain on the track; the wire boundary fence still on the left, trees still on both sides. The somewhat sunken track may be overgrown along this section in which case climb out of it to the right and walk alongside it. On reaching another gate, leading into the field on the left, ignore it but continue straight ahead on the main track (probably still overgrown) alongside the fence, trees still on both sides of it.

Good views still of Black Mixen and the Whimble behind. Pedwardine Wood is ahead in the right foreground while the hills beyond it are those above Bucknell – that with fields part of the way up to its wooded top is Bucknell Hill, the wooded hill to its left is Bucknell Wood. Below Bucknell Hill part of the settlement of Bucknell may be just visible.

On a very clear day there are tantalising glimpses to be had, left, on the far horizon beyond the hills bordering the Teme valley (such as Bucknell Hill) of the tops of the higher hills of south Shropshire, such as Corndon Hill (513 metres/1683 feet), Stiperstones (536 metres/1759 feet) and the Long Mynd (516 metres/1693 feet).

At the far boundary of the field the track reaches a double metal farm gate with a small stile to its left. Cross this into the next field, the track now becoming less distinct and no longer sunken. The accompanying trees and wire fence also come to an end here. Go straight ahead across the field from the stile.

Crossing the field look half-left ahead to see the 'summit' of Harley's Mountain with its triangulation point (386 metres/1266 feet). Nearing the far side of the field superb views open up right, left and behind. Virtually all of the hills already mentioned as being visible on this section of the walk may now be seen. Behind, the observatory can still be seen on its hill top site.

On reaching the far side of the field pass through another metal farm gate and proceed straight ahead, the wire fence boundary of the new field on the immediate right.

Crossing the new field views open up ahead, with Titterstone Clee Hill visible behind the twin ridges of Mortimer Forest. The long wooded mass of Shobdon Hill Wood dominates the right foreground while, on a very clear day, the entire chain of the Malvern Hills may be visible half-right ahead – over 30 miles distant. Reaching the far side of the field, the twin summits of Brown Clee Hill – Abdon Burf (540 metres/1772 feet) and Clee Burf (510 metres/1673 feet) – come into view half-left ahead, ie. to the left of Titterstone Clee Hill.

The track is now more distinct again. Remain on it as it passes through another metal farm gate and continues to follow the right boundary through the next field to another metal farm gate (SO348689). Passing through this gate bear half-right to follow the right boundary hedge of the field so entered, descending slightly, the track now indistinct and reduced to path width.

The low wooded hills visible in front of Mortimer Forest, directly ahead, are the Wigmore Rolls. Look left/half-left on a clear day for a distant view of Leintwardine. If the sun is shining on the village then the church tower there will be particularly prominent – almost golden in colour. Again, on a very clear day, the Malvern Hills may be seen, now straight ahead on the far horizon.

Where the boundary hedge – on the right – bends away to the right continue straight ahead across and down the field to its far boundary hedge. On reaching this turn right to follow it down to the corner of the field. Here pass through a gap (old gateway) into the next field and continue to follow the hedge, which is on the left – the track now wide and distinct once more. A group of old farm buildings will be seen ahead on the left – named as Mountain Buildings on Explorer Map 201 (SO352686).

Remain on the track as it leaves the field through a double metal farm gate. Continue straight ahead ignoring an arm of the track which leads left to the farm buildings. The track gains a metalled surface and just after passing the buildings bears left and then right to pass through another gateway into a field. As the initial left bend begins – just past the buildings – leave the track to walk straight ahead over rough ground towards a gateway through a boundary hedge ahead (the metal farm gate here is likely to be open).

Passing through the gateway there is an immediate choice of footpaths in the new field. Take the path which goes almost half-right from the gate down the field (the other path goes straight ahead down the left hand boundary hedge). **❻**

Walking down through this field, Shobdon Hill Wood is now directly ahead while the small settlement of Lingen, the end of this stage of the walk, appears below in the foreground. The church will be seen to the left hand side of the settlement.

Head almost half-right diagonally down the field to a stile at the bottom, situated just to the left of a large ash tree (itself the left of two isolated large trees in the field boundary). Crossing this head straight down the field ahead to a pronounced dip in it and then, on reaching this, bear slightly left up towards farm buildings adjacent to the far left hand corner of the field – Mynde Farm on Ordnance Survey maps.

On reaching the corner of the field by the farm buildings pass through a double metal farm gate in the boundary on the left and walk alongside a barn (on the right as it is passed). Passing the far corner of the barn bear very slightly right (almost straight ahead) to reach a gateway through a boundary fence ahead. Through this bear half-right, around a small disused quarry area (on the right). Continue in the same direction to descend through a metal farm gate into another field.

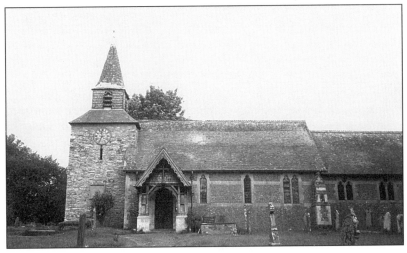

Lingen Church

Ignore a well used track bearing half-right towards woodland but instead go straight ahead from the gate down the field to a stile at the bottom. Cross this and go straight ahead down the next field, keeping a wire boundary fence on the left about 20 yards distant all the way down. (Note: Explorer Map 201 shows the footpath on the far side of this fence but this is not the case.) On reaching the bottom of the field cross a stile in the bottom boundary, situated a few yards in from the corner of the field – NOT the stile over the boundary on the left which is adjacent to it.

The stile gives access onto a muddy track. Turn right along this but then, after about 20 yards, go left through a gateway into the corner of a field, a corrugated metal farm building on the immediate right. Follow the left hand boundary hedge of this field to its far left hand corner and cross a stile there into another field. Here again follow the left hand boundary hedge to the corner where the footpath bends to the right around a small corrugated metal building. Pass through a metal farm gate which is situated alongside and to the right of this building and immediately to the left of the corner of a garden bordered by fir trees.

Entering the next field through the gate walk along its right hand boundary – the boundary with the aforementioned garden – to its far right hand corner. Here pass through a metal farm gate onto a road. Turn left along the road. On reaching a T-junction, by Turn Farm, turn right. Walk along the road, past some old cottages on the left. After about 100 yards the road bends right. As it does so maintain direction by leaving it, left, for a footpath which leads into Lingen churchyard.

Lingen Church

Although the current church of St. Michael & All Angels dates only from 1891 there has been a building on this site since the thirteenth century. The original church of this period was replaced by a new building in the seventeenth century, during the reign of James II, and so the current church is the third recorded here.

Stone for the current building was quarried on the nearby Harley estate at Brampton Bryan. The stone parts of the tower were retained from the seventeenth century structure as were some of the internal timbers and benches. The roof of the nave was replaced in 1953 after a fire.

Outside on the south wall of the church tower is a large tablet which, with the church clock, was erected in memory of the local First World War dead. Four names are listed – William Jones, William Frank Jones, John Edward Morgan and Frederick Williams – although a quick search of the tombstones in the graveyard quickly yields a fifth – Sergeant Isaac Jones. The oldest legible tombstone inscription hereabouts dates from April 1700.

The turning is underneath three large trees – two horse chestnuts and a sweet chestnut. Follow the path to the church porch. ❼

If not going into the church, turn right at the porch to follow another path through the churchyard and out through the lych-gate onto the road. Turn left along the road. At a road junction remain on the 'main' road which bends right and is signposted to Presteigne and Kington. The Royal George public house is about 100 yards further along the road on the left and this stage of the walk ends here.

Lingen

Lingen is a small, sleepy settlement, set well off the major through routes of the area. It is thought to take its name from the stream which flows through it, Lingen being an old Celtic brook name meaning 'clear stream' or 'sparkling water' (some add 'in a dark place'). Probably dating from Saxon times, at the time of *Domesday Book* (1086) it was held by Thurstan of Wigmore. A castle here, situated to the north of the present church, was never more than a wooden structure. Its mound survives.

The descendants of Thurstan took the name of Lingen in the reign of Richard I. The most famous member of the family was Henry Lingen who fought on the Royalist side in the Civil War and whose troops were among those involved in the unsuccessful siege of the castle at Brampton Bryan, held for the Parliamentary cause by Lady Brilliana Harley. He was knighted by King Charles I in 1645 but was later captured by troops under Colonel Birch and imprisoned at Hereford. Escaping, Sir Henry later held Goodrich castle for the king until Charles himself was captured in 1646. Lingen surrendered in June of that year but lived to see the Restoration of the Monarchy in 1660.

An earlier member of the family, Sir John, fought on the successful Yorkist side at the battle of Mortimer's Cross (1461). He is buried in Aymestrey Church.

Less than a mile to the south-east of Lingen is Limebrook Priory which was founded around 1190 by Ralph de Wigmore, a descendant of Thurstan. An Augustinian nunnery, it was dedicated to St Thomas of Canterbury. Suppressed at the time of the Dissolution of the Monasteries under Henry VIII, the priory was disused by 1539 and fell into ruin. Only one wall remains standing today although it is likely that the nearby sixteenth century Limebrook Cottage incorporates materials from the building.

The Royal George is now the only pub in Lingen. The building dates from 1723 and legend has it that it incorporates timbers from the ill-fated ship of the same name which sank at moorings off Spithead with the loss of all 800 crew, a disaster which is the subject of a well known poem by William Cowper which begins ;

Toll for the brave...
The brave that are no more,
All sunk beneath the wave,
Fast by their native shore.

Unfortunately for this legend the ship sank in 1782, some 59 years after the pub was built, so that unless the timbers were used in some subsequent rebuilding work on the premises the story is unlikely to be true.

On the end wall of the building is an old round yellow Automobile Association sign proclaiming that it is 5¼ miles to Leintwardine, 5¼ to Presteigne and 152¼ to London. Whatever happened to precise mileages on road signs?

Modern Lingen has few facilities of any great use to the walker apart from the pub and even this has limited opening hours – evenings only on weekdays, all day at weekends. There is a telephone box outside the pub.

Further along the road through the village from the pub, and slightly off route, is Lingen Nursery and Gardens which are open to the public and incorporate a small tea room. Opening hours are daily 10 a.m. to 5 p.m., February to October.

Stage 5

Lingen to Leintwardine

Mileage: 13 Miles (From Lingen: 3 miles to Lower Lye; 5 miles to
Wigmore; 9½ miles to Adforton)
O.S.Maps: 1:50000 (Landranger): 137 (Ludlow);
1:25000 (Explorer): 201 (Knighton & Presteigne); 203 (Ludlow)

This is the longest of the eight stages which make up the complete walk.

*The route leaves Lingen alongside Lime Brook before climbing east
through woodland. A combination of tracks, footpaths and finally a road
section take it into the small settlement of Lower Lye where it turns north
towards Wigmore.*

*The route to Wigmore is shared with one of the loop walks from the
Mortimer Trail. It is mainly over track and field path. Wigmore, a village
of formerly far greater importance than now, is visited after which a short
climb takes the route past the ruins of the castle, once home to the
powerful family of Marcher Lords, the Mortimers.*

*The route then crosses the wooded hills of the Wigmore Rolls, via forest
tracks and paths, before descending to the small settlement of Adforton.*

*A short ridge walk takes it to the site of Wigmore Abbey. Thereafter the
way is fairly level to Leintwardine, initially along quiet roads but latterly
over field paths, alongside the River Teme.*

STARTING outside the Royal George P.H., facing the road, turn left.
After about 40 yards on the road, just before the small bridge over
Lime Brook and by Brook House, turn left onto a footpath which
crosses the road at this point. Passing through a metal farm gate walk
alongside the wire boundary fence – on the right, with the garden of
Brook House beyond it.

Continue along the fence to reach the banks of Lime Brook (also on
the right) and walk alongside this for about 30 yards before crossing it
via a small culvert. Over the brook, bear left to follow it on a narrow
path with a wire boundary fence on the right. The path runs under trees
– mainly hawthorn.

After another 40 yards cross a stile over the wire boundary fence on
the right and turn left along a path which immediately crosses the brook
via a wooden footbridge. (A right turn over the stile leads to the rear
entrance of Lingen Nursery which has a tea room – see note at Stage 4,
page 54 for details.)

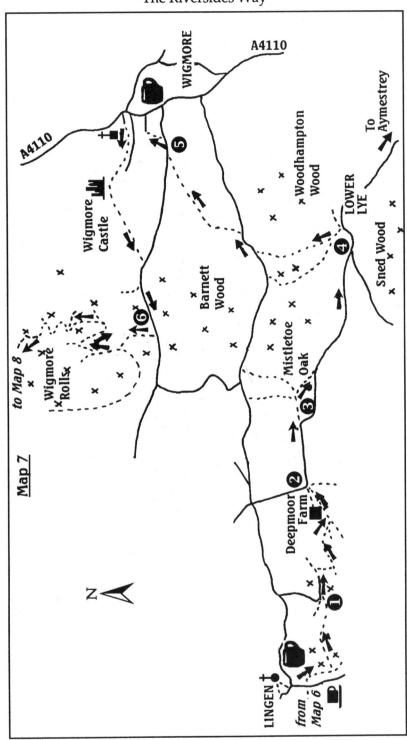

Map 7

to Map 8

Wigmore Rolls

Wigmore Castle

Barnett Wood

WIGMORE

A4110

A4110

† ⑤

⑥

Woodhampton Wood

LOWER LYE

Sned Wood

To Aymestrey

④

Mistletoe Oak

③

②

Deepmoor Farm

①

LINGEN †

from Map 6

N

Over the brook, continue alongside it on the narrow path – a wire boundary fence on the left, the brook on the right. Another wooden footbridge takes the path over a side stream, the confluence of the two just to the right. A third wooden footbridge carries the path across a seasonally wet area and almost immediately to a T-junction with a wider path.

Turn right along the path, a wire field boundary fence on the right and woodland to the left. After about 120 yards, where the path widens at a junction, take the left arm – a track which climbs up into the woods (SO368667).

Climb up the fairly steep track through the woods. At a junction, part of the way up, ignore the track going right but continue straight ahead. Bending slightly to the right, and still climbing, the track reaches the edge of the wood where a stile leads into a field. Head very slightly left up the field – towards its top left-hand corner where it meets more woodland. Here pass through a gateway and go straight ahead, descending slightly on what is initially a clear track but which soon becomes less distinct.

Passing through a gap in an incomplete wire boundary fence the obvious track underfoot finally disappears. Continue ahead, gradually bearing very slightly left to follow the contour of the land through the large field, heading for a far boundary of trees. Further across the field aim to pass just to the right of a couple of small hawthorn trees – and then through a metal farm gate in a wire fence.

Crossing the large field look back over the left shoulder for a good view of Harley's Mountain which was crossed on Stage 4 of the walk.

Nearing the aforementioned tree boundary head for a wooden farm gate through it, situated near the far right-hand corner of the field. Approaching this the track underfoot re-establishes itself. Cross a stile situated just to the left of the gate and walk the 15 yards or so needed to reach a tarmac track (SO375669). **❶**

Turn right down the initially steep track which bends left and, after about 100 yards, loses its surfacing, running under trees and between wire fences. A stream accompanies the track on the right. After a further 140 yards (that is 240 yards from the point where the tarmac track was first reached) leave the track, right, for a footpath which drops down to cross the stream. The junction is waymarked with a Mortimer Trail Circular Walk sign and a blue bridleway sign, both on a marker post.

Crossing the stream, via a rough wooden footbridge, ignore a metal farm gate straight ahead but instead bear left up a narrow path – again marked with a Mortimer Trail sign. The path climbs up through trees away from the stream. Pass through a wooden gate at the top of the initial climb and continue straight ahead on a slightly sunken path between trees, climbing gradually.

On reaching a junction with a track bear left up this, again as indicated by a Mortimer Trail marker post. Climbing beneath trees, about 30 yards after the junction/marker post pass through a metal farm gate in a wire fence across the track. Continue climbing the obvious track. Passing through another metal farm gate it narrows to footpath width. Through a third metal farm gate it emerges onto a stony farm track. Turn left up this.

On reaching a T-junction with a similar farm track turn left (SO380667). Walking along this track, farm buildings should be visible to the left – Deepmoor Farm. When the stony track makes a right-angled bend left to head towards the farm leave it by continuing straight ahead on an obvious track, initially with a dirt surface but soon becoming grassy underfoot. It runs along between hedges, mainly of hazel. It eventually reaches a metal farm gate, a wooden gate to the left bearing Mortimer Trail logos. Pass through the latter to emerge onto a stony track. Turn right along the track.

Before turning right along the track look over the gate to the left and along the stony track to Deepmoor Farm. There is a good view back to Cole's Hill, in the foreground, with Lingen Vallet Wood to its right. Framed between the two in the far distance are the hills of Radnor Forest, with the Whimble prominent. Half-right is Harley's Mountain.

The stony track emerges onto a road (SO384670) on a bend – with another stony track going off to the right at the same point. Turn right along the road (almost straight on in fact). It is initially level and straight. ❷

Walking along the road, the wooded hills to the left are the Wigmore Rolls, crossed later on this stage of the walk. Half-left the two ridges of Mortimer Forest are visible, that on the right being High Vinnalls – 370 metres/1214 feet. Just visible over the top and beyond this is the summit of Titterstone Clee Hill. The rounded wooded hill directly ahead in the middle distance is Woodhampton Wood.

Still fairly straight, the road begins to descend – undulating downwards in a succession of dips. When it makes a 90 degree bend right to drop more steeply down past a house leave it, at the start of the bend, by continuing straight ahead down a grassy track. After about 275 yards on this straight track leave it, right, on a footpath which goes over a stile situated next to a metal farm gate (SO393672) and underneath two large ash trees on the left of the track and a large oak on the right of it – the area hereabouts is, in fact, named as Mistletoe Oak on Ordnance Survey maps. (A footpath goes off the track to the left here as well.) ❸

Lingen to Leintwardine

Over the stile into a field, bear half-left towards a corner of the hedge boundary opposite. Rounding this corner follow the boundary down the field until it bends away again right, a row of trees on the left. Here bear left to follow the line of trees, keeping them on the right. Aim just to the left of a post carrying overhead wires, passing under these as the field is descended. Passing through an incomplete tree boundary enter another field and bear half-right diagonally down this to a stile at its bottom corner, just to the left of a metal farm gate and adjacent to a stream. This gives access onto a road.

Turn left along the road, crossing the stream. The quiet road meanders along making an overall sweeping bend to the left and passing a disused quarry area *en route*. After about three quarters of a mile it passes the first houses of the small settlement of Lower Lye.

The long wooded hill to the right during the latter stages of the road walk into Lower Lye is Sned Wood. The route of Stage 1 runs along the other side of it, through Aymestrey gorge.

At a road junction ignore a turning right. Passing through the settlement of Lower Lye, on the right of the road is the large black and white building of Lye Court, with a large black clinker-built wooden barn on either side of it. About 220 yards after the road junction, just past the second of the black barns, the road makes a marked bend to the right (SO406669). At the start of this bend, by the corner of the barn, leave the road, left, to walk up a track. ❹

By remaining on the road a walk of just over 1½ miles leads to a T-junction with the A4110 road at Aymestrey, with a right turn and short walk over Aymestrey Bridge leading to the Riverside Inn (Start of Stage 1/Finish of Stage 8).

By using this link, in either direction the eight stage circular walk may be split into two separate circular walks, as follows:

(1) Aymestrey – Presteigne – Bleddfa – Knighton – Aymestrey (Using Stages 1 to 4 and Stage 5 to the point above and then the road link to Aymestrey): About 39½ Miles in total.

(2) Aymestrey – Leintwardine – Ludlow – Richards Castle – Aymestrey (Using the road link to Lower Lye and then Stage 5 from the point above, and Stages 6 to 8): About 35½ Miles in total.

Ignore a footpath going off right, through a gate into a field, a few yards up the track but continue on it, soon beneath trees and in a cutting. The track climbs and bends to the right. At a fork in it take the right option. Becoming more grassy underfoot the track runs between high hedges, of mainly hazel, and begins a gradual descent.

The Riversides Way

Where the hedge on the right allows it look across the small valley to the right to see the buildings of Woodhampton Farm nestling below the wooded hill of the same name. One of the buildings houses the small brewery which supplies the Riverside Inn at Aymestrey and several other local hostelries.

Eventually the grassy track reaches a metal farm gate into a field with a stile to the left of it. Cross this and turn immediately right, as indicated by the Mortimer Trail sign, to follow the contour of the land through the field, initially skirting above a group of four oak trees. Crossing the field maintain height and aim towards the lower near corner of woodland ahead. Cross a stile which is situated just below the corner of the wood.

In the next field bear gradually right, again maintaining height and passing just below two oak trees. Keep well to the left of a single tree in the middle of the field – again an oak. Passing this tree head towards the right-hand boundary where the field ahead narrows and follow this along to the far right-hand corner of the field. Here cross a stile, situated to the left of a metal farm gate, to emerge onto a quiet road.

The rounded wooded hill to the right of these fields is Woodhampton Wood. The woodlands starting to the left are Oakley Hill Wood and Barnett Wood. All are privately owned and managed.

Turn right along the road. After about 360 yards on it, at the end of a bend to the right and where the woodland on the left of the road ends, leave it by taking a footpath on the left. This departs the road over a stile which is accessed through quite a thick hedge and is again signposted as a Mortimer Trail Circular Walk. Head half-right up the field so entered to its top right-hand corner. Here cross a stile, to the left of a gate, and immediately turn right to follow the boundary of the new field along. Nearing the far corner of the field bear slightly left to a stile over the boundary ahead, situated to the left of a metal farm gate about 30 yards in from the corner of the field. Cross the stile into the next field.

Glorious views ahead as this field is entered. Straight ahead are the two ridges of Mortimer Forest. In the middle foreground, to the right of these, the long wooded hill is Gatley Long Coppice.

Head half left from the stile down the field towards woodland beyond its bottom left-hand corner. On reaching a wire boundary fence, ahead, turn half-left to walk along it and then cross it via a simple wooden stile, about 20 yards before the corner of the field. Over this, turn left to continue along the fence and then drop down, slightly to the right, to cross a seasonal watercourse via a wooden footbridge.

From the footbridge bear half-right to climb gradually up and across the new field. Aim to keep just above a succession of large trees dotted across this field. Maintaining direction, head towards a group of trees forming part of the far boundary where a stile giving access onto a road will be found. The stile is situated just to the right of a metal farm gate.

Crossing the latter part of the field look right to see the wooded hills below Bircher Common and Croft Ambrey, with its hill fort, crossed on Stage 8 of the walk. The long flat-topped wooded hill to the right of these is Yatton Hill. To the left of all of these, and much nearer, is Gatley Long Coppice.

Crossing the stile there is a first glimpse of Wigmore church ahead. A good crop of giant puffballs was found growing near the stile when we walked this way in mid August.

Turn right down the road. After 100 yards on it, as it begins to bend to the left, leave the road for a footpath on the left which climbs up through the hedge and over a stile (SO412688).

Over the stile, the village of Wigmore suddenly comes into view ahead and below. A few steps further on look half-left for the first view of the ruins of Wigmore Castle.

From the stile go straight ahead across a track to follow a hedge boundary, which should be kept on the immediate right. Follow the hedge down a rough meadow area until reaching a stile through it. Turn right to cross this and then follow the narrow path beyond, hemmed in on both sides by hedges.

More good views of village, church and castle from this path and the descent which follows.

The uneven ground to the left of the path through the meadow, before the stile onto the narrow path, marks the former site of Wigmore Abbey, situated here for only twelve years, between 1160 and 1172. The steep narrow path from here down to the lane (Brook Lane) is that up which the monks had to carry their water supplies and their complaints about the hard climb are recorded in documents of the time. The path is known as 'Jacob's Ladder'.

The narrow path makes a bend to the left downhill and becomes very steep. An attempt has been made to cut steps into it. Follow it down to where it emerges onto a grassy/dirt track (Brook Lane) and turn right along this. Ignore a footpath going off left but continue to follow the track which becomes stony, as the first dwellings of Wigmore are passed, and eventually emerges onto the main road through the village – the A4110. Do not cross the road but instead turn left along it.

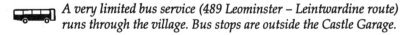

A very limited bus service (489 Leominster – Leintwardine route) runs through the village. Bus stops are outside the Castle Garage.

Walk along the pavement of the A4110 for about 100 yards and then take the second turning on the left – a narrow lane indicated as leading to the church and castle. (Note: The first turning on the left, just

Wigmore

Formerly of far greater importance than it is now, Wigmore is a fairly large village situated astride the busy A4110 road. The Romans had a camp to the east of the present settlement, on what was the western branch of Watling Street and there was also an important Saxon fortress here. There is some disagreement as to the origin and meaning of the name of the modern settlement. In Saxon times it was known as Wisingamene or Wigingamere, meaning either Wicga's or Wega's moor or possibly deriving from the Saxon words 'wigge', meaning 'warrior', and 'mere', meaning 'pool' or 'great water'. Another suggestion is that the name comes from the Welsh 'Gwig Maur', meaning 'big wood' while yet another has it derived from a nearby Danish camp and meaning 'The moor of the Sons of War'. A final opinion has it derived from the Old English words 'wicga' and 'mor' and meaning 'quaking marsh' – not unlikely given the flat, marshy lowlands which would have been left behind when the former lake here drained away after the last ice age.

By the time of *Domesday Book* (1086) Wigemore, as it was then known, was held by Ralph de Mortimer and it was under this family of powerful Marcher Lords that the settlement came to exert far wider influence. For the four centuries following the Norman Conquest the history of the area is inextricably linked with that dynasty and their castle above the village.

With the move of the main Mortimer power base to nearby Ludlow Castle and the end of the direct male Mortimer line both castle and village became of less national importance although still a significant local focal point. After the Local Government Act of 1894 Wigmore became the headquarters of the Wigmore Rural District Council, a situation which lasted until 1930 when that council merged with Leominster and the administration centre moved to that town. Since then the village has become more of a 'backwater' although it remains a centre for education, with a large modern school.

There is plenty of accommodation to be had in and around the village – with several guest houses, farmhouse accommodation, a small hotel/restaurant (The Compasses) and a public house (Ye Olde Oak Inn) all offering rooms.

The village has a small store and a sub post-office/shop. There is also a garage. Several small craft centres have bases here including a woodcarver/furniture maker, a second furniture maker, and a pottery.

There is a telephone box just to the right of where the route reaches the A4110. A very informative History Trail leaflet to the village is available, free of charge. Copies can often be obtained in the sub post-office.

opposite the pub – Ye Olde Oak Inn – is Castle Street which has an information board about the castle at its entrance.)

Walk up the short lane to the churchyard – less than 50 yards. Enter the churchyard via a wooden gate and follow a narrow grassy path along its left-hand boundary hedge to reach the entrance porch of the church (see box on page 64).

Continue along the narrow grassy path beyond the church porch to exit the raised churchyard down a short flight of steps. Go straight ahead up a stony/partly-metalled track which climbs past the last few dwellings out of Wigmore, narrowing to become a grassy path. There is a lane down to the left – the continuation of Castle Street.

Remain on the obvious narrow, grassy path as it passes through a kissing gate and skirts some grassy mounds, on the right, which probably represent the site of the original wooden castle or the remains of siege-works. The path now takes on more of a compacted dirt surface and is confined between two wire fences. Through another kissing gate, a farm on the lane down to the left, the path passes an English Heritage notice board – 'Saving the Castle'.

Continue to follow the path straight ahead. It runs along the left-hand boundary fence of a wide grassy platform, below the castle, to a point where the grassy platform narrows, another fence approaching from the right. Here the path drops down a short slope to reach two kissing gates, that on the right leading to the castle ruins (see box on page 66).

There are good views to be had from the grassy area below Wigmore Castle. Looking right from the route of the walk, and working from right to left, Gatley Long Coppice and both ridges of Mortimer Forest are visible. Directly to the right on the far horizon the prominent spire belongs to the church of St. Giles, Downton. The long hill with the thin line of trees across the top of it is Tatteridge Hill. Leintwardine lies to the left of this but is not visible.

On a clear day those with keen eyesight may just be able to make out the church at Burrington. It lies to the right of the Downton spire, in front of the end of the left ridge of Mortimer Forest, and is situated much lower.

To the left of and below the wooded slopes of Gatley Long Coppice the settlement of Leinthall Starkes may be seen. Again, those with keen eyesight may be able to make out the sails of the windmill above the settlement. In summer these may be hidden behind trees but there is a better opportunity to see them, from a higher vantage point, during the climb after the castle.

In the foreground Wigmore Cemetery and chapel are prominent. They date from 1899. Beyond and to the left of these the house with the row of poplar trees alongside is Gotherment. Look beyond this to see the Grange, which incorporates the remains of Wigmore Abbey and is passed later on this stage of the walk.

Wigmore Church

The church of St. James, Wigmore, was founded by the Mortimer family on the site of an earlier Saxon building – the circular churchyard on high ground suggesting a religious site of some age, probably Celtic or early Dark Ages. The building possesses a very early Norman nave with herringbone masonry visible on the north wall outside (at its western end). The tower, chancel and south aisle, and its roof, are fourteenth century while the north chapel and nave roof are fifteenth century in origin. The pulpit is early sixteenth century, with fine wooden linenfold-panelled sides. The font is fourteenth century. An internal window in the south wall of the nave is Norman and was an external aperture before the south aisle was built.

A medieval altar has been reused as a window sill in the tower while there is a tomb of a seventeenth century vicar of the church –

Churchyard Cross, Wigmore

Alexander Clogie – under the present high altar. Very much a real life 'Vicar of Bray', Clogie was vicar under Charles I, the Commonwealth, Charles II, James II, and William and Mary, surviving all the changes from High Church to Puritanism and back again. The inscription on his tomb reads 'Here lyeth, in hope of a glorious resurrection unto life eternal, the body of that holy, reverend, and learned divine, Mr. Alexander Clogie, who departed this life 24 Oct. 1698, aged 84, Minister of Wigmore 51 years.'

Just inside the entrance to the church, in the south aisle, is a stone carved with a fine cherub-head. Outside, the base of the churchyard cross is fourteenth century; the remainder of later date and much restored. The churchyard was closed for burials in 1901, a new cemetery, just to the north along the A4110, having been opened in 1899.

The dedication of the church is to St. James the Less – he is depicted in the stained glass window in the south wall of the chancel – rather than to the other apostle of the same name who was venerated at nearby Wigmore Abbey.

Pass through the left-hand of the two kissing gates to continue on a narrow path, confined by the wire fence of the castle grounds on the right and a wooden handrail on the left, a track beyond this.

Pass through another kissing gate to join the track on the left. Proceed straight ahead along the track, bounded on both sides by fences and bushes, to enter the bottom corner of a field through a farm gate (SO408692). The short section of track can be very muddy after wet weather.

Go straight ahead up the steep field towards a group of trees which will be seen near its top boundary, passing the corner of a paddock area, on the right, *en route*.

Climbing the steep field look behind for good views of the castle ruins and across the Vale of Wigmore beyond. There are similar views to those obtained from the grassy platform below the castle, with the sails of the windmill at Leinthall Starkes, below Gatley Long Coppice, now more likely to be visible.

On reaching the group of trees (ash) pass beneath them, continuing in the same direction to reach the top boundary of the field. Bear right to walk along this. Passing another ash tree, on the right, ahead will be seen a gate through the boundary, a stile to its right. Cross this to enter the next field and climb straight ahead – roughly towards the further of two poles carrying overhead wires which will be seen as the field is entered. Nearing the pole bear slightly left to reach a farm gate and stile in the top corner of the field. Cross the stile into the next field. Here follow the left hand boundary for about 35 yards to reach a stile, to the left of a metal farm gate, which leads out onto a quiet road.

Wigmore Castle and the Mortimers

The earliest reference to Wigmore is in the Anglo-Saxon Chronicle for AD921and refers to a fortress of King Edward at Wigingamere. This castle or fortification later withstood a Viking attack. It appears likely that the fortifications here were begun by Ethelfreda, daughter of Alfred the Great, early in the tenth century. Remains of large earth banks running north-east from the present castle can be traced to this day and probably represent part of this Saxon stronghold.

At the time of the Norman Conquest Wigmore was held by Edric, the Saxon Earl of Salop. After 1066 it passed to William Fitz-Osbern, Earl of Hereford and it was he who had a wooden castle built on the site between 1068 and 1071. The grassy mounds below the current castle are possibly the site of this original Norman fortification, although there is also a theory that these are the remains of siege-works dating from the 1155 action (see below).

In 1074 William's son, Roger de Breteuil, fell out of favour with the king, after he had joined in a revolt against him, with the result that the castle was forfeited to the Crown and granted to Ralph de Mortimer in 1075. Thus began Mortimer power in the area.

In the twelfth century – under Hugh Mortimer – a stone keep was built further west of and higher than the wooden castle and this was extended and new stone buildings added right through to the fourteenth century. Initially many of the new buildings and defences would still have been of timber however, with the first rebuilding in stone effectively completed by 1246, under Ralph Mortimer.

In 1996 a kitchen dating from the twelfth century building was discovered under the present remains of the south wall, during work to secure the site by English Heritage.

The castle was captured several times during its early history. In 1155 the forces of Henry II took it from Hugh Mortimer and in 1191 a force loyal to Richard I took it from Hugh's son Roger when he joined the rebellion of Prince John. Both occasions illustrate the growing threat felt by the Crown in the face of the increasingly powerful Mortimer dynasty.

From 1246 Roger Mortimer – (like most noble families of the time the Mortimers limited themselves to a few favourite Christian names, in their case Roger and Edmund) – fought in the long, bloody campaigns against the Welsh under Llywelyn ap Gruffyd. In later years he supported Henry III against Simon de Montfort. The castle was again besieged at this time but was still in Mortimer hands in 1265 when Prince Edward (the future Edward I), sought refuge there after escaping from Hereford. A story tells that Roger fought at the Battle of Evesham, where the rebellion was finally crushed, and that as a reward for his services to the king he was given the head of de Montfort as a trophy which he sent home to his wife at Wigmore. What the lady in question felt about this is not recorded! (As with most stories of this nature historical accuracy has probably been lost over centuries of retelling. A similar tale concerns Roger Mortimer and the head of Llywelyn ap Gruffyd, the recipient on this occasion being the king, and the possibility of the two events having been confused cannot be overlooked. All that is certain is that those were violent times!)

It was another Roger Mortimer (1287-1330), who was created First Earl of March. Although such powerful nobles served a useful purpose for the Crown in that they kept the peace in the troubled borderlands they could also be the source of potential rebellion and claims to the throne themselves if they became too powerful and this is exactly what happened in the case of the Mortimers. For the next 100 years or so the family played a major role in England's history.

It was the same Roger Mortimer who married Joanna de Geneville, a member of the de Lacy family, and so secured possession of Ludlow Castle which thereafter became the main Mortimer power base. He also undertook a further rebuilding of Wigmore Castle – in the form recognisable from the ruins seen today.

It was Roger, again, who plotted against Edward II. By 1322 he was a prisoner of the king in the Tower of London but escaped and fled to France where he became both ally and lover of Edward's estranged wife, Isabella – known as the 'She Wolf of France'. In 1326 the couple returned to England and deposed Edward, themselves then ruling in the name of his son, Edward III. When the latter came of age he had Roger executed. As a result of Roger's treason the family lost the Earldom of March and the castle at Wigmore. These were granted instead to William Montacute but were regained for the Mortimer cause when Roger's grandson, another Roger, married Montacute's heiress in 1354.

By the early fifteenth century another Mortimer was plotting against the Crown. Originally intending to quell a Welsh uprising under Owain Glyn Dwr, Edmund Mortimer (uncle of another Edmund, fifth Earl of March, and acting head of the dynasty at the time as his nephew was only 11 years old), was instead captured at the Battle of Pilleth (1402) and held to ransom. Annoyed at Henry IV's delay in arranging his freedom – probably a deliberate ploy on the part of the king as the Mortimers themselves had such a strong claim to the throne – Edmund agreed to marry Glyn Dwr's daughter, Catherine, and join the Welsh leader in the so called Tripartite Indenture – the third party to it was Henry Percy, Earl of Northumberland – with the intention of overthrowing the king and splitting the country into three amongst themselves. The planned combined uprising failed to materialise however. Edmund Mortimer continued to support Glyn Dwr and died defending Harlech Castle in January 1409.

In 1415 Richard, Earl of Cambridge made an unsuccessful attempt to seize the throne from Henry V on behalf of Edmund Mortimer, Fifth

Earl of March, his brother-in-law, on the grounds that the Mortimers had a stronger claim to the throne – Edmund being descended from the second son of Edward III while Henry was only descended from the third son. Richard was executed for his part in the plot but Edmund and his brother Roger were spared. They were however imprisoned and later banished to Ireland.

Edmund's death in Ireland in 1425 spelt the end for the Mortimer dynasty as there was no surviving male heir. Wigmore and the Earldom of March passed to Richard, Duke of York – the son of Richard, Earl of Cambridge and Anne Mortimer, sister of Edmund (Fifth Earl of March).

It was Edward, the son of Richard (Duke of York), who was to give Wigmore a final taste of glory for it was from the castle that he rode out to the Battle of Mortimer's Cross (1461) which effectively ended the Wars of the Roses in favour of the Yorkist cause, Edward then becoming king (Edward IV). The castle then passed to the Crown.

Although eclipsed in importance by Ludlow, the castle continued to be occupied and from the reign of Elizabeth I was rented by the Harleys, of Brampton Bryan. This family bought the castle in 1601. Supporters of the Parliamentarian cause in the Civil War, the Harleys had the castle fortifications dismantled in 1642 to prevent the Royalists seizing it for their own use. Thereafter the castle buildings fell into disrepair.

After a long period in private ownership the castle ruins had fallen into such disrepair as to be unsafe. In 1995 they were given to the Nation by its then owner, John Gaunt, a local farmer, and English Heritage were asked to make the ruins safe and to run the site. The ruins of the castle were reopened to the public on 12th October 1999.

Turn right along the road which immediately begins to descend. At a slight bend to the left ignore a stony track going off to the right but remain on the road which soon enters woodland, the descent becoming steeper.

At the bottom of its long descent the road crosses a deeply incised stream and begins a gradual climb. Just under 100 yards beyond the stream crossing – and after about 800 yards in total on the road – leave the road on the right to take a stony track which leads past a name-sign for the Forestry Commission's Wigmore Rolls woodlands. **❻**

Walk up the track, passing a wooden barrier designed to prevent vehicular access. The stony track climbs gradually and bends slightly to the left. On reaching a T-junction with another forest track turn right along it, (SO396690).

(Note: A left turn at this junction takes the walker onto the main western perimeter track of the Wigmore Rolls Forest which is used by the Riversides Way in its later stages. If unable to follow the route as described below – because of tree felling for example – then retrace the route to this junction and take the left option to use the perimeter track instead, rejoining the Riversides Way at **❼** below.)

The new track almost immediately bears right and is initially fairly level. After the initial right bend it straightens and then, after about another 200 yards, bears left and begins to climb. At the start of this left bend, at a Y-junction, take a less distinct track which goes right. After a little under 100 yards on this track, (just after crossing a small culverted stream), at another Y-junction, turn right onto a stony track which bends right and immediately begins to climb steadily.

At the top of its initial climb the track makes a very sharp bend to the left, (SO397692). About 15 yards after this bend ignore a track going right at a Y-junction but continue on the main track which begins to meander and, after an initial gentle climb, undulate through the forest.

The climb up the track and the subsequent meander through the forest may provide something of interest for amateur fossil hunters.

Remain on the track. A succession of minor bends right and left follow. About 400 yards after the sharp bend and Y-junction, at another Y-junction of sorts, ignore a logging track which goes up to the right in favour of the stony main track which itself commences a more marked right bend at this point. A significant left bend follows and then another to the right. At the apex of another left bend ignore an indistinct path which goes right.

Walking nearby one frosty December morning I had what remains my eeriest and closest encounter with native wildlife. Pausing to watch a nuthatch performing acrobatics on a tree a movement seen from the corner of my eye caused me to glance along the track where a fox was standing, about 10 yards from me and watching me intently. The two of us stood and stared at each other for what seemed like minutes before I decided to see how close it would let me get to it. I had halved the distance between us before it nonchalantly turned and trotted away along the track.

Beyond the left bend the track begins a short descent. Another right bend follows and then, bending left again, the track begins to climb and reaches what was, at the time of writing, a more open area within the forest – the scene of tree-felling over recent years.

A good place for spotting deer. Thanks to the kindness of the Forest Enterprise staff at Ludlow I was the first walker to be allowed onto the Wigmore Rolls after the Foot & Mouth epidemic of 2001 and my progress through the woodland to this point was rewarded by numerous sightings of deer, not used to seeing people hereabouts after some months of the forest being closed.

A fairly straight section leads to a junction with another track, at a sharp bend on the latter. Here go right.

Now, nearing the top of the main ridge of the Wigmore Rolls, depending on tree cover views to the west begin to open up. The familiar rounded mass of Harley's Mountain – crossed on Stage 4 – may be seen slightly left ahead.

The track bends left and then right, climbing to reach a triangular track junction at the ridge-top, within 100 yards. Here go left.

The section of track which follows may be lined with dozens of orchids in season. Admire but PLEASE DO NOT PICK OR UPROOT THEM.

After an initial straight and level section – of about 100 yards – the track begins to bend left. Part of the way around this long bend – about 200 yards in total after the triangular junction – locate an indistinct junction on the right of the track and leave it here, (SO389697).

Having turned off the track (right) immediately – at a Y-junction of sorts – go half-left along a narrow path. (The option which goes half-right here is an indistinct track. Note that Explorer Map 201 shows the path which is taken as being a significant track while Landranger Map 137 does not show it at all! The truth is somewhere in between: the path is narrow and sometimes quite overgrown but remains distinct.)

The narrow path runs generally straight and level over the crest of the ridge and then descends fairly steeply down its western side to a junction with the main western perimeter forest track, (SO386696). Turn right along this. **❼**

Harley's Mountain is directly ahead in the distance during the last stage of the descent to the junction with the main perimeter track. During the subsequent walk along the perimeter track, where gaps in the tree cover allow, there are superb views over to the west to Harley's Mountain and, to its right, Pedwardine Wood and Brampton Bryan Park. Further along the track the low wooded mass of Coxall Knoll and the high hills along the far side of the Teme valley – Hopton Titterhill, Bucknell Hill, Bucknell Wood and Stow Hill – also come into view.

Follow the main perimeter track which meanders and undulates along to eventually pass through a metal farm gate, leaving the Wigmore Rolls Forest, and reach a quiet road. Turn right up this, (SO392710).

The road initially rises and bends right but soon levels out and commences a straighter section, eventually meandering and undulating along.

Views from the road are initially restricted by high hedgerows but soon the two main ridges of Mortimer Forest become visible half-left ahead – the right-hand ridge is High Vinnalls, (370 metres/1214 feet), the highest point in the forest and with a fire hut at its summit. The northern end of the Vale of Wigmore is in the foreground.

At a junction ignore a road going left but continue straight ahead. The road now begins a gentle descent and soon passes the first few dwellings of the small settlement of Adforton – the charmingly named 'Christmas Cottage' soon followed by the picturesque 'Laburnum Cottage' and 'The Green', (the latter thatched), all on the left.

Continue down the road to reach a junction with the busy A4110, a small car park – with seat – and the church of St. Andrew just to the right, (SO402711).

(Option: An alternative approach to St. Andrew's church is to turn right off the road just opposite 'The Green', down what is signed as a Public Bridleway but is initially the stony drive to a half-timbered dwelling. On reaching the near corner of the dwelling turn left to follow a path which initially runs between high banks but then crosses and follows a stream (left). It emerges onto a track on a right-angled bend. Go straight ahead along this track which, within 20 yards, becomes metalled and in a further 100 yards reaches the A4110 road with the church immediately on the right.)

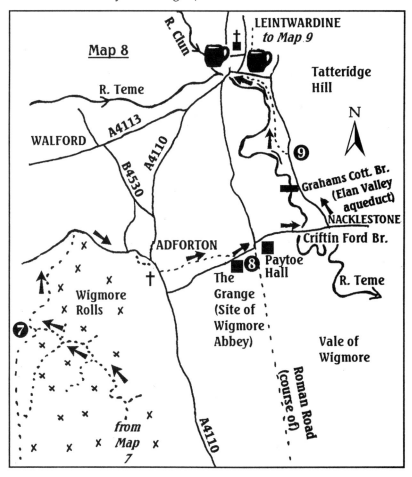

The church of St. Andrew, Adforton was built as a chapel of ease for Leintwardine parish in 1875.

There is a telephone box by the entrance to the churchyard.

Turn right along the road – taking great care as it can be very busy! After about 100 yards, with Old Bank Farm on the right and an old Primitive Methodist Chapel on the left, (across the road), cross the road with care to leave it up a steep tarmac drive on the left, just beyond the chapel.

As the drive makes a sharp bend left continue straight ahead, leaving the drive to cross a stile, to the left of a farm gate, into a field.

From the stile head slightly left up the field, heading towards a pole carrying overhead wires which will be seen at the top. Cross a stile situated just to the left of the pole to enter another field.

Good views while climbing the field. Looking right down the Vale of Wigmore the line of poplar trees at Gotherment are prominent but, on a clear day, there are views right down the Vale to the hills of Croft Ambrey and Yatton at its southern end. Working left from these Gatley Long Coppice and the windmill at Leinthall Starkes should be visible. Looking left the low round wooded hill is Coxall Knoll, which has an Iron Age hill fort at its summit. Behind it may be seen the higher hills behind Bucknell – Bucknell Hill, Bedstone Hill and Hopton Titterhill.

In the new field bear very slightly left from the stile – although keeping the left hand field boundary some distance away. Maintain this direction and when a wire boundary fence appears on the right walk to this and follow it through the long field.

Despite its height above the surrounding land there are initially no views to be had from this ridge. This is due to the top of the ridge on the left and trees beyond the boundary fence to the right. Soon, however, the rounded Tatteridge Hill – recognisable by the thin line of trees across its top – comes into view directly ahead. Where there are gaps in the trees on the right there are superb views down the Vale of Wigmore to be had. The sharp-eyed may just be able to pick out the ruins of Wigmore Castle on the slopes of the Wigmore Rolls.

On reaching a metal farm gate through the boundary on the right pass through it to leave the field. An obvious broad grassy track descends from the gate through a rough, partly quarried area, towards the buildings of the Grange/Wigmore Abbey which will be seen just ahead below. Follow the track down. It passes below outcrops of rock and small quarries and above some large farm buildings. Reaching the bottom, bear right to pass through a wooden double farm gate and out onto a quiet road (SO409714). Turn left along this (the entrance to the Grange/Wigmore Abbey is just along the road to the right). **❽**

Walk along the road. When it makes an almost 90 degree bend to the left, after about 350 yards, ignore a substantial track going right – the course of the old Roman road (an arm of Watling Street) – but remain on the road. About 70 yards further on, and with a house called 'The Olde Granary' on the left, at a road junction turn right – signposted 'Ludlow, Burrington' (SO413716).

On the right, a few yards along the new road, is the rambling black and white, half-timbered Paytoe Hall. Across the road from it is a large pond.

Wigmore Abbey

Wigmore Abbey, or Priory, was founded on this site by Hugh Mortimer in 1179 – Hugh laid the first foundation stone and Brian de Brampton, (of Brampton Bryan), the second – although it was Hugh's chief steward, Oliver de Merlymond, who did most to establish the religious community. Initially based at Shobdon, (1140), and later at Aymestrey, (on the site above the Riverside Inn), on first moving to Wigmore the foundation occupied the site passed earlier on this stage of the walk, (between 1160 and 1172). It was an Augustinian order and was dedicated to St. James and St. Victor.

The foundation was heavily supported by the Mortimer family, many of whom are buried on the site – including five Earls of March. In the mid nineteenth century a stone coffin containing a body and an urn containing ashes were found.

There is also reputedly a tunnel leading from the Abbey buildings to Wigmore Castle. In 1870 a subterranean passage, some six foot in height and wide enough for four men to walk abreast through, was discovered. While some regard this as being evidence for the existence of the tunnel to the castle others dismiss this idea on the grounds of the distance between the two buildings – one mile – and see the passage as possibly a large sewer for the Abbey. Evidence of another underground passage – this time leading in the direction of Paytoe Hall – was discovered in the cellars in 1935, giving rise to the theory that Paytoe Hall may once have been a nunnery. Some years ago a man fell into an underground passage outside the stables at the Grange, again this leading towards Paytoe.

Dissolved during the reign of Henry VIII it is thought that some of the stone from the Abbey buildings was subsequently reused, (1540), for the church arcades at Aymestrey. What is more certain is that its fifteenth century carved wooden misericords, choir stalls and benches were saved and taken to the church of St. Mary Magdalene at Leintwardine, (passed on Stage 6 of the walk). The remains and ruins of the Abbey – which include architecture from the twelfth though to the sixteenth centuries – were incorporated into the later Grange which still occupies the site. Unfortunately this is privately owned and not open to the public.

The half-timbered gatehouse formerly bore a plaque which listed the thirteen known Mortimers buried on the site and gave a brief history of the Abbey. It read:

'In this Abbey lie the remains of the noble family of Mortimer who founded it in 1179 and who ruled the Marches of Wales for 400 years. Ralph 1140. Hugh 1185. Roger 1215. Hugh 1227. Ralph 1248. Roger 1282. Edmund 1318. Roger 1330. Edmund 1331. Roger 1360. Edmund 1381. Roger. Edmund. The Abbey, covering several acres, was destroyed by the Welsh 1221, rebuilt by Edmund about 1370, was finally destroyed by King Henry VIII 1538.'

The hall is twelfth century in origin. There is a theory that it may once have been a nunnery. In 1935 when signs of a secret passage leading towards Paytoe were discovered at the old Wigmore Abbey site corresponding bricked up remains were discovered here.

There is a good view of the windmill at Leinthall Starkes to the right along the initial stage of the new road. Tatteridge Hill is slightly left ahead and the sharp-eyed may be able to make out a small blue brick and concrete structure on its slopes which is a valve chamber for the Elan Valley Aqueduct.

Walk along the quiet road. It is initially straight but then bends slightly to the left and then right before returning to its original straight course, between high hedges. Bending slightly right, about 1000 yards after the junction, the road reaches Criftin Ford Bridge over the River Teme (see box on page 75).

Over the river, continue along the road which rises to a junction at the small farming settlement of Nacklestone – about 350 yards beyond the river crossing. Here turn left, signposted 'Leintwardine'.

Walking the new road, Tatteridge Hill is immediately to the right – the valve chamber of the Elan Valley Aqueduct now much more prominent. On the left, where gaps in the hedgerows allow, are views across to the river.

Walk along the quiet road. After an initial brief descent it levels out and meanders along between high hedges, soon commencing a long bend to the left. About half a mile after the junction a short low section of wall with a stile above it replaces the hedge on the right while on the left of the road a small wooden gate leads into a field and the Graham's Cottage Bridge crossing of the Teme by the Elan Valley Aqueduct. Remain on the road.⋆

The stile on the right gives access to the valve chamber seen on the slopes of Tatteridge Hill. Through the gate on the left is another valve chamber and, beyond that, the Aqueduct crossing of the river.

The four pipes of the Elan Valley Aqueduct run for 73 miles from the Elan Valley dams, in mid Wales, to Birmingham and have carried the water supply for that city since construction of the project between 1892 and 1904.

There are three crossings of the River Teme en route, of which Graham's Cottage Bridge is the first – the other two being at nearby Downton (Downton Bridge), and Ludlow (Steventon Bridge), the latter of which is passed on Stage 7 of this walk.

A 128 mile, 10 day walk based on and along the course of the Aqueduct is the subject of my book, 'The Elan Valley Way', published in 1999 by Meridian Books.

Continue along the road. After about another 450 yards, and just beside the first of a line of poles along the left-hand side of the road (carrying overhead wires) take a footpath which leaves the road on the left, through a kissing gate, to drop down into a field (SO414728). **9**

From the kissing gate head half-right across the field, aiming between a very large oak tree (right) and the banks of an abandoned river channel (left) and following the line of the foot of the original slope down from the kissing gate.

Approaching the far boundary of the field bear slightly left towards a line of willow trees, which mark the course of another old river channel, to reach another kissing gate to the right of a metal farm gate in its far left hand corner. Passing through this again follow roughly the

The River Teme and Criftin Ford Bridge

The River Teme rises in the Kerry Hills of Powys, in an old disused quarry on the slopes of Bryn Coch, just north of Cilfaesty Hill, and flows generally east or south to join the River Severn just below Worcester, a total length of over 75 miles. On the way it accepts the waters of several important tributaries – the Clun (at Leintwardine), the Onny (at Bromfield), the Corve (at Ludlow), and the Rea (at Newnham Bridge).

It is thought that the Teme may have originally flowed northwards beyond where Leintwardine is now situated but that it became trapped by ice at the end of the last Ice Age and, after flooding what is now the Vale of Wigmore, cut a new channel eastwards – now Downton Gorge. The section of the river which includes Criftin Ford Bridge is characterised by sweeping bends and abandoned channels. It is known variously as Leintwardine Fishery or Nacklestone Oxbows.

Criftin Ford Bridge is an idyllic spot. Pausing here on a sunny October afternoon I saw a heron and swans, and shared a late lunch with a flock of ducks on the river.

The simple single-span bridge is a tasteful 2000 replacement for a much older (and weaker) design formerly quite common on both Teme and Lugg in this part of Herefordshire. One such bridge was crossed on Stage 1 at Kinsham – if that also has not already fallen victim to improvement or replacement to cope with heavier loads.

same direction – initially along the foot of the slope in the field and then keeping the boundary fence to the left about 20 yards distant as the foot of the slope bends away right.

Crossing this field, the tower of Leintwardine church makes its first appearance ahead. Beyond the abandoned channel, on the left, the main river is now much nearer.

Maintaining the same general direction, approach the boundary on the left and walk along it – the river now just beyond. Passing a redundant stile continue to follow the fence, a small farm settlement (Trippleton) and the recently vacated road across the field to the right.

Continue to follow the fence as it bows out in a long sweeping bend – caused by it following the banks of yet another abandoned river channel. At the end of the long bend walk past another redundant stile, continuing to follow the fence with the main river alongside again.

On reaching another fence ahead (SO407736) turn right to walk along this, heading towards an enclosed area which houses a small sewage/recycling plant.

Pass through a kissing gate in the fence (left) and bear right to maintain direction along it. After only another 15 yards the path swings left away from the fence to cross a slight depression in the ground – where it appears part of a hedge boundary has been removed – and enter the adjacent field where it swings right to follow a hedge boundary (right) along. On reaching the aforementioned recycling plant that hedge boundary is replaced by a high fence. Continue to follow it past a redundant kissing gate.

The tower of Leintwardine church is half left ahead.

The footpath emerges through a small wooden gate (to the right of a wooden farm gate) onto a quiet road (Rosemary Lane). Turn left along it into Leintwardine, past the fire station on the left and the Sun Inn and a fish and chip shop (the Fiddler's Elbow) both on the right. Ignore a road on the right (Watling Street) and on reaching a T-junction cross over the road to the Lion Hotel, where this stage of the walk ends.

A limited bus service runs through the village, to Ludlow or Knighton. There is a bus stop opposite the Lion Hotel.

My arrival in Leintwardine late one sunny October afternoon was greeted by the sight of a heron flying under the arch of the old bridge over the River Teme.

Leintwardine

Leintwardine represents that most unusual of settlements, a Saxon village built on the exact site of a Roman garrison town. The Saxons were a superstitious people and generally regarded it as unlucky to build over previous remains. In this instance however the importance of the site, on high ground above the confluence of the Teme and Clun, appears to have outweighed their fears.

The Roman fort and settlement here – known as Bravonium or Branogenium – was established around AD160 at the point where the Roman road of Watling Street crossed the Teme. The settlement was rectangular in layout and surrounded by a wall and ditch. Watling Street ran to the immediate east of the wall. The present main street, High Street, runs north-south through the middle of the site.

The name 'Leintwardine' is of Saxon origin and means the 'enclosure on the River Lent'. The Lent was the old name for the River Clun – of Celtic origin, meaning 'torrent' or 'stream'.

The Saxon king Edward the Confessor owned the 'Hundred' of Leintwardine (Lenteurde), which extended into more modern Shropshire, Herefordshire and Radnorshire and contained forty-nine manors at that time.

By the time of *Domesday Book* (1086) the manor of Leintwardine was under the control of the powerful Mortimers of Wigmore Castle, one of some 130 manors given to Ranulph (Ralph) de Mortimer by William the Conqueror in return for his support.

Seen from a distance the large village is dominated by the buff sandstone tower of the church of St. Mary Magdalene (see separate note at Stage 6), which seems to glow almost golden on sunny days.

Leintwardine has a fish and chip shop (The Fiddler's Elbow – passed in Rosemary Lane on the way into the village), a post office cum store, a petrol station with shop, a general store (on Watling Street), a butcher, and a very small HSBC bank branch with limited opening hours – two days per week as of the time of writing. There is a public phone box 100 yards or so up the High Street from the Lion Hotel, outside the bank.

The village has three public houses. There is the Lion Hotel by the bridge over the Teme (recalling the lion on the Mortimer coat of arms), and at the far north of the village is the Cottager's Comfort – known as 'the Poker' or 'the Poker and Hole' by some of the village's older residents. Finally, along Rosemary Lane – and passed as our route enters the village – is the Sun Inn, a real old-fashioned alehouse with no frills or pretensions.

Stage 6

Leintwardine to Ludlow

Mileage: 9½ Miles (From Leintwardine: 4½ miles to Bringewood
Forge Bridge; 6½ miles to Bromfield)
O.S.Maps: 1:50000 (Landranger): 137 (Ludlow);
1:25000 (Explorer): 203 (Ludlow)

The route climbs out of Leintwardine using paths and tracks in the main. After briefly touching the busy A4113 road it enters the more peaceful Downton Estate, mainly on metalled tracks, before dropping down into Downton Gorge at Bringewood.

Riverside and field paths take it next to Bromfield, with its sad church. It then turns south-east towards Ludlow, passing through the landscaped surroundings of Oakly Park en route and eventually approaching the town along the Teme, below the castle walls, to reach Dinham Bridge.

The stage ends with a climb up Whitcliffe Common for the classic view of Ludlow, with Titterstone Clee Hill forming the backdrop to the Castle and Church of St Laurence. From here the route descends through woodland to cross the river via Ludford Bridge and so enter the town.

STARTING outside the Lion Hotel cross the road (High Street) to gain the pavement opposite and turn left up it. Just past the telephone box and HSBC Bank branch, take the first turning on the right (Church Street). The church (*page 80*) is on the left-hand side of it.

On reaching the T-junction at the end of Church Street turn left. Cross the road (Watling Street) and after about 30 yards – opposite a small general store/off-licence – turn right along a lane. Where this ends there is a small children's play area accessed via a gate on the right while ahead is a metal farm gate with two stiles to its left – one over the fence straight ahead and the other over a fence, left.

Take the latter of these options to enter a field. Having crossed the stile turn right for about 10 yards, to round the corner of a garden to the left, and then turn left to follow the fence of this and other gardens along, a boundary hedge soon establishing itself. On reaching the corner of the field cross a stile into the next. Continue to follow the left boundary hedge through this field until reaching a corner formed by the boundary fence of a school, ahead. Ignore a footpath going left here (over a stile next to a gate in the corner) but instead turn right to follow the school boundary fence along.

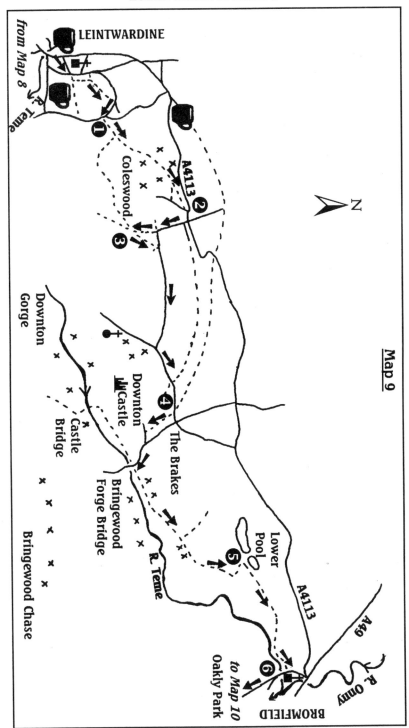

Walk along the school boundary fence until reaching the corner of its grounds. Here continue in the same direction, passing through an incomplete boundary of hawthorn trees ahead. Maintain direction across the field to reach a stile at its far boundary. Cross this into the next field and bear half-left, roughly towards a house which lies within its own fenced-off grounds within the field and more specifically to a simple wooden footbridge over a watercourse which is situated opposite the end of the house. Cross the footbridge and again bear half-left, to maintain direction, aiming towards a red metal farm gate in the far corner of the field which has a stile to its left. Cross this stile onto a quiet road and turn right (SO407746).

Almost immediately, at a Y-junction with a track, go right – remaining on the road. At a road junction ignore a road going sharp left but continue straight ahead. A further 80 yards along the road leave it, left, through a metal farm gate and along a track – as indicated by a bridleway sign (SO411745). **1**

The stony track climbs gradually, a small stream in a gully down to its left. After about 280 yards it makes a 90 degree bend to the right. Here leave it, left – effectively straight ahead – through a large metal farm gate and into a field, as indicated by a bridleway sign. (Note: The track beyond the bend is signed as a public footpath.)

The walk up the track from the road can be quite idyllic, with a firm surface underfoot and the small stream alongside. I spent an interesting few minutes here, one fine October morning, watching grey squirrels chasing each other up, down and around the large trees hereabouts.

Follow the left boundary hedge up the field – the slight depression alongside the hedge may contain a small stream – towards woodland at the top. On reaching the top of the field pass through a gap in the incomplete boundary of trees there, situated about 20 yards in from the top left hand corner, to enter another field.

Leintwardine Church

The church of St. Mary Magdalene, Leintwardine, stands just inside the original eastern wall of the Roman settlement of Bravonium (or Branogenium). Built on Saxon and Norman foundations the current building is of mainly thirteenth and fourteenth century origin with 1865 rebuilding. The oldest visible part is a blocked doorway in the west wall of the nave which is twelfth century. The church is mentioned in *Domesday Book*.

The tower of the church is thirteenth century and was built as much for defence as any other reason – with walls up to six feet thick. It is seventy-six feet in height and there is a spiral staircase of 103 steps to the top. A chamber at the second stage of the tower was once home to Thomas Shelve, a hermit, who had previously resided in the small chapel on Ludford Bridge – see note on page 130.

The top storey of the tower contains the eight bells of the church. The tenor bell bears the inscription 'I to the church the living call. I to the grave do summon all'.

Inside the entrance porch to the church is a peculiar iron grille which looks as if it might have been used as some form of punishment but in fact is to prevent anyone from standing under the weights of the church clock and meeting with an accident.

The old clock of the church may be seen preserved inside. Made of wrought iron and brass and with two crude stone weights it worked

Old clock mechanism in Leintwardine church

only one hand on a slate dial which is now hidden under the stucco and later dial on the tower outside. It is one of the oldest of such mechanisms in the country, dating back to at least the early sixteenth century. Also in the church is an octagonal fourteenth century font on a more modern base.

Standing at the steps leading from the nave to the chancel look at the base of the arches left and right to see carved heads of King Edward III and a lady, possibly his wife Philippa. In 1328 Roger de Mortimer set aside the income from some of his lands to pay for nine chaplains to say mass daily, in the church, for the souls of himself, his wife Countess Joan, his mistress Isabella (known as the She Wolf of France because of her numerous political intrigues – such as with Roger against her own husband Edward II), Isabella's son Edward III, and his wife Philippa.

The unusually great difference in floor levels between the nave and chancel is down to the church being built upon the old Roman embankment. Roman bricks and tiles have been discovered below the floor of the building.

In 1181 Hugh de Mortimer had given the church to the abbey he had founded at Wigmore (passed on Stage 5 of the walk). At the time of the Dissolution (1538) the carved wooden misericords, choir stalls and benches of the Abbey, dating from the fifteenth century, were brought to the church where they can still be seen. The misericords are very similar to the better known examples in St. Laurence's Church in Ludlow but have suffered far more damage.

Outside, in the churchyard, is the grave of General Sir Banestre Tarleton. The son of a Liverpool draper, Tarleton purchased a commission in the Kings Dragoon Guards and fought in the American War of Independence, rising to the rank of Lieutenant Colonel and earning such a reputation in the eyes of his American foes that he became known as 'Bloody Tarleton'. His role in the war has recently been portrayed, in a very unsympathetic light, in the Hollywood film *The Patriot* which starred Mel Gibson.

Returning to England as a hero after the war, Tarleton became a close friend of the Prince of Wales eventually taking on a mistress – the actress Mary Robinson – of whom the Prince had grown weary and living with her for five years. In 1798 he was promoted to Major General and married the daughter of the Earl of Alcester, Susan Priscilla. The couple left London and moved to Leintwardine, living at Leintwardine House. Although distant from the capital Tarleton remained friends with the Prince of Wales and would sometimes send him gifts of salmon which he had caught in the River Teme.

Tarleton died in 1833. There is an imposing monument to him in the Mortimer Chapel of the church – a marble tablet surmounted by laurel wreath, helmet, breastplate and sword and with an eloquent eulogy – erected by his wife.

In the new field bear initially slightly left and then follow the right-hand boundary up it - woodland alongside. Bridleway signs continue to point the way. The field is long and narrow and bends slightly right. Woodland beyond the far (left) boundary hides the busy A4113 road.

Climbing up through this field look behind for a good distant view of the tower of Leintwardine church and distant hills beyond it - Pedwardine Wood and Harley's Mountain (old friends from Stage 4 of the walk!)

Nearing the top of the field bear slightly left to forsake the right boundary fence and to reach a farm gate midway along the top boundary. Pass through this onto a stony track and into woodland. The track climbs steadily through the woods (Coleswood).

The traffic noise from the A4113 becomes much more noticeable as the climb continues and the road gets much nearer. Thankfully the tree cover masks much of the noise and all but a fleeting glimpse of vehicles.

Deer seen hereabouts one sunny October morning.

Remain on the track as it continues to climb and meanders beneath the mainly deciduous trees. At a Y-junction (SO418753), where the main track (right) bears right and begins to climb more steeply, take the left option - a slightly lesser track, and less stony, which continues the gradual climb now along the edge of the woodland. A bridleway sign points the way at the junction.

The dirt track continues to climb steadily, a stream down to the left in a small gully at the very edge of the trees. Remain on it until it reaches the top of its climb at a T-junction with another track. Turn left along this, almost immediately reaching the A4113 road. ❷

Turn right along the road. Cross it as soon as it is safe to do so - to take advantage of the wide grassy verge on that side of it. After about 70 yards on the road re-cross it to turn right off it, through a metal farm gate (which may be open) and up a metalled farm track. (A similar track goes left off the road at the same point.)

Walk up the steep straight track - ignoring another track which goes left off it after only about 15 yards.

While climbing turn around and look half left behind for views of the hills behind Bucknell - Bucknell Hill, Bedstone Hill and Hopton Titterhill. As more height is gained other hills further up the Teme Valley appear.

Continue up the metalled track. Still straight, it reaches the top of its climb and levels out. Soon it begins a very gradual descent and reaches a 'crossroads', with metalled tracks ahead and to the left and a dirt track going right (SO426749). Go straight ahead here.

Within a few yards the track loses its metalled surface, becoming stony. About 180 yards beyond the crossroads (and about 50 yards before a house ahead on the track), a footpath crosses. Turn left onto this, through a double metal farm gate (alongside a garden) into a field. ❸

Entering the field there are superb views directly ahead of both Brown Clee and Titterstone Clee Hills and the north-west ridge of Mortimer Forest – the latter often referred to as Bringewood Chase. Follow the right hand slope of Titterstone Clee Hill down to where the nearer left hand slope of Bringewood Chase 'meets' it to pick out Ludlow, with the tall tower of the church of St. Laurence prominent.

Entering the field turn half-left to walk down it. (Do NOT follow the obvious track along its right hand boundary.) A line of wooden stakes across the field marks the way if the field is under crops. Head diagonally down the field towards a group of trees beyond its bottom corner.

Walking down the field look right for a sighting of the spire of the church at Downton (St. Giles). Look further to the right for a view down the Vale of Wigmore, past Gatley Long Coppice towards Croft Ambrey.

I experienced a very wet crossing of this field one otherwise fine October day – with cabbages and maize, both quite high and soaking with dew. Fortunately for navigation purposes the farmer had the stakes in place!

At the bottom of the field the footpath drops down onto a grassy track. Turn left along this to soon emerge onto a metalled track. Turn right down this (SO427749).

Walking down the metalled track, the spire of Downton Church is still visible to the right while ahead, half right, the tower of the church of St. Laurence at Ludlow is already much more prominent.

Continue down the fairly straight metalled track. On reaching some large farm buildings, on its left, it makes a sweeping bend to the right.

The long range of wooded hills prominent half right ahead is Bringewood Chase – the more north-west of the two main ridges of Mortimer Forest. Just after passing the large farm buildings the church tower at Ludlow is directly ahead.

The metalled track eventually descends to a T-junction with a quiet road. Turn left along this, a wooden signpost at the junction indicating 'Brakes Farm'.

The route has been on Downton Estate land for some time, hence the oak signposts indicating the way to the various farms and other locations hereabouts – a feature of the Estate. They do NOT indicate that a right of way exists. In fact there are very few public rights of way through the Estate.

Downton Castle lies just under half a mile to the right from the road but is hidden by trees.

The road descends, passing isolated dwellings *en route.* Ignore tracks going off either side of it (the one on the right marked 'No Right of Way' and the one on the left indicated as being a public footpath) but remain on the road which shortly passes a telephone box. The road bends left and then sharp right, crossing a stream (Stone Brook) – a house called Stonebrook Lodge on the right.

At the end of the right bend the road levels out and begins to meander along, the stream down to its right in a deep gully. A house on the right stands alongside a fine stone bridge over the stream – one of the entrance lodges to Downton Castle. Ignore a track going left, signposted 'Brakes Farm', and another going right to 'The Orphanage' but remain on the road. Not long after these turnings a large house on the left, 'The Brakes', is passed and the road bends slightly left. ❹

Within 100 yards of 'The Brakes' a footpath crosses the road (SO449753). Leave the road, right, via two stiles to enter a field. From the stiles head very slightly left across and down the field, passing about 40 yards to the right of a cottage as the far boundary is neared – and just to the right of an old well in the field. Nearing the far (bottom) boundary head for the left corner of the field, a second cottage adjacent to it, where the path passes through a gap and out onto a quiet metalled track.

Turn left along the track, past the aforementioned cottage. Beyond this the track bears right and descends to a T-junction. Here turn right, down another metalled track – the noise of water becoming noticeable ahead. The track descends past a house called 'Forge Cottage', on the left, to reach a fine single arch stone bridge over the River Teme (Bringewood Forge Bridge) with a semicircular weir just above it (SO454749).

The river is here just downstream of Downton Gorge. The area hereabouts is called Bringewood and was an early ironmaking centre at several forges. Walk out onto the bridge and look upstream (right) for a glimpse of part of the buildings of Downton Castle and the spire of Downton church (St. Giles) beyond.

Unfortunately there is no public right of way along the whole length of Downton Gorge but for those wishing to take a closer look at the castle there is a footpath along the river below it from Bringewood. To follow this turn right off the metalled track just before reaching the bridge.

Do not cross the river but instead leave the metalled track as it bears right to approach the bridge, turning left along a track. (A footpath leaving the metalled track on the right here runs along the riverbank below Downton Castle.)

Follow the obvious track along the fast flowing river, through woodland. Passing the ruins of an old building, by rapids in the river,

Bringewood Forge Bridge, a stone variation on the famous Iron Bridge at Coalbrookdale

Downton Castle and Estate

Downton Castle was built by Richard Payne Knight between 1772 and 1778. A member of the iron-founding dynasty, he was something of a scholar, anthropologist and archaeologist but also, more importantly, a leading light of the Picturesque Movement which denounced the formal landscaping of the likes of Capability Brown in favour of a wilder and more natural approach. At Downton, one might argue, Nature had done most of the hard work for him as regards the castle grounds. The River Teme, its waters trapped at the end of the last Ice Age, has cut a spectacular gorge just upstream of the castle. Knight added walks, caves, tunnels and fine bridges across the river.

Downton church (St Giles) stands in a field, at the end of a long vista from the castle. It was built to replace an earlier building – also dedicated to St. Giles – which stood about half a mile further south-west, at Downton on the Rock, and was abandoned in 1861. Its architect was Samuel Pountney Smith.

Bringewood Forge Bridge was built in 1772 as part of Richard Payne Knight's landscaping of Downton Estate. It was designed by the Shrewsbury architect Thomas Farnolls Pritchard, also responsible for the Iron Bridge at Coalbrookdale, who is supposed to have based it on his plans for that more famous structure.

Iron-founding on Bringewood Chase

Iron-founding started here in about 1600, using locally produced charcoal and iron ore and limestone from the Clee Hills, brought in by packhorse. In 1690 Job Walker purchased the lease of the works, having previously operated it for the Earls of Essex and Craven, and Francis Walker purchased Downton Estate in 1716. The Walkers sold out, in1727, to the Knight family who also owned furnaces at Wolverley and Madeley.

Several members of both Walker and Knight families are buried in Burrington churchyard – on the other side of the ridge across the river – and lie under cast iron grave slabs manufactured here.

Iron production reached its peak here in the first half of the eighteenth century after which the area was overtaken by technological advances at developing Coalbrookdale. Iron-founding ceased at Bringewood in the latter years of the century and there is little evidence on the ground now to recall its former significance.

At the peak of its production there were no fewer than fourteen water wheels in action along a mile of river here – the highest concentration of water power in England at that time.

the track bears left and begins to climb away from the riverbank. Passing through a gateway it reaches a clearing. Go slightly right across this to cross a stile into a field.

Entering the field the route leaves Herefordshire to enter Shropshire.

Walk straight ahead from the stile following the contour across the field – along the top of the final slope leading down to the riverbank, below right. Continue to follow the contour, bending slightly left with it and aiming to pass just to the right of and below a single large oak tree and a large patch of gorse beyond. Passing these head for the remains of a metal wind pump ahead. Pass this, to its left, and maintain direction to locate a largely redundant stile over an incomplete boundary fence ahead. It is situated just to the left of a metal farm gate.

From the stile head half left across the next field, towards a single large oak tree. Aim to pass just to the left of this and then maintain direction up a steep slope towards the far boundary where there is a stile, situated just to the left of woodland (SO461758).

Good views behind across to Bringewood Chase (Mortimer Forest) while climbing the slope to the stile. Those with an eye for that sort of thing may be able to trace the line running through the woodland on a level which marks the course of the Elan Valley Aqueduct across it.

Cross the stile, and immediately another, into the next field. Here follow the right boundary fence, the aforementioned woodland (Stocking Nursery) beyond it.

Crossing this long field one October afternoon I surprised a fallow deer – a stag with a magnificent set of antlers – which proceeded to run along ahead of me for almost the entire length of the field before jumping the fence to the right and disappearing into the woods.

On reaching the far corner of the very long field turn left to walk down its far boundary. At the bottom corner turn right to cross two stiles into the next field. Follow the left boundary of this – another very long field. There is initially a large pond beyond the boundary fence – marked on Explorer Map 203 as Lower Pool. ❺

Crossing this field, Titterstone Clee Hill makes a reappearance half right ahead. This field and the one previous are of an unusual length compared with most hereabouts. The two of them measure over a mile, and that is without the walk down their common boundary!

Continue to follow the left boundary across the field. On reaching the corner bear right, along its far boundary for about 50 yards to a double metal farm gate. Pass through this into the next field. On entering the field walk straight ahead from the gate for about 15 yards and then turn right to walk along the edge of the field, trees beyond the boundary on the right.

The small settlement of Bromfield, its church tower prominent, appears across the field.

Follow the boundary with the trees beyond it to reach banks of the River Teme. Bear left to walk along the river, still following the edge of the field. The river is initially beyond a wire boundary fence and trees. On reaching the end of the field cross into the next via a stile situated to the right of a metal farm gate, alongside the river. Continue to follow the riverbank path through the new field – no longer with a fence between it and the river. Bromfield Bridge, spanning the river, will be seen ahead. On reaching it cross a stile at the left end of its parapet to emerge onto a metalled drive (to Oakly Park).

If visiting Bromfield church or the Clive Arms public house, or if intending to catch a bus in the village, turn left along the drive but to continue the walk turn right and cross Bromfield Bridge.

Bromfield takes its name from the large amounts of broom which once grew hereabouts, literally meaning 'the Field of Broom'. The settlement grew up just upstream of the confluence of the Rivers Teme and Onny.

The Onny is the river beyond the church. Beyond that is the A49 road which may be reached by continuing along the drive past the church. The Clive Arms restaurant/public house, a small village shop, telephone box and bus stop are a little way along the busy road.

Across Bromfield Bridge, over the Teme, the large building half left by the river was a corn mill.

Leintwardine to Ludlow

 Buses on the 738-740 Ludlow – Leintwardine – Knighton routes stop outside the Clive Arms on the A49 in both directions of travel.

Having crossed the river, via Bromfield Bridge, continue along the metalled drive. Within 60 yards the drive splits, at a Y-junction, with the two arms passing either side of a small gatehouse to Oakly Park. Go right, to enter the park through metal gates. **❻**

Oakly Park became the seat of the Herbert family after they had abandoned the old Bromfield Priory site – damaged after the fire of 1638. The estate later passed to the Clives and the Windsor-Clives and is now the property of the Earl of Plymouth. Both the Herberts and the Clives were very active in the politics of Ludlow, representing the borough in Parliament on many occasions during the seventeenth and eighteenth centuries.

Oakly Park House is situated along the left arm of the drive from the gatehouse and can just about be seen from the route of the walk. The present house dates from the early eighteenth century but was much altered in 1800 and again in 1820. It is a large brick structure with prominent Tuscan columns.

Follow the metalled drive through the landscaped parkland, large fields to the right and Oakly Park House to the left. Ignore a metalled track going left to the hall, not quite half a mile after the gatehouse, but continue ahead on the drive, now beneath mature trees.

A spotted woodpecker seen here one fine October afternoon.

Bromfield Church

The church of St. Mary the Virgin, Bromfield, stands between the Rivers Teme and Onny. An earlier church on the site, possibly dating from about AD900, is mentioned in *Domesday Book* (1086). A Norman church, parts of which survive in the present building, was built here early in the twelfth century and in about 1135 a Benedictine Priory was founded.

The Priory buildings were adjacent to the south wall of the nave of the church. It is thought that an original central tower of the Norman church either collapsed or was dismantled at some point and was replaced by a new tower, at the north-west corner of the church, in the early thirteenth century.

The priory was dissolved in the reign of Henry VIII, probably in 1538. After lying empty for some twenty years or so the old Priory buildings were bought by Charles Foxe who converted them into a house – the chancel becoming a dining room with a bedroom above it. The nave of the church remained in public use as a place of worship.

In 1638 a fire destroyed the house, although the church was saved. The chancel had also survived and was given back to the church in

---

1658 by Richard Herbert – the Herberts had acquired the property via marriage into the Foxe family. It was at this time that the plastered rounded ceiling of the chancel was painted with cherubs floating among clouds – completed in 1672 by Thomas Francis at a cost of seven guineas. Even after some 300 years this remains spectacular but is best described as 'naive' art and may not be to everyone's taste.

The masonry of the nave survives from the original Norman church, as do some arches from the original central tower. The present tower and the north aisle are thirteenth century in origin. The font is fourteenth century. The nave possesses an oak roof dating from 1577 and which was only revealed when the church was restored in 1890, having previously been concealed under plaster.

Outside to the west is the fourteenth century gatehouse to the Priory – of stone with a timber framed upper floor. It has recently been restored by English Heritage and the Landmark Trust. Against the south wall of the church are the ruins of Foxe's House – currently unsafe.

Sad to say but at the time of writing the church itself is suffering from serious structural problems and is full of scaffolding and rarely used. In 1997 a routine inspection revealed that one end of a roof beam had been eaten away by rot and that death-watch beetles were active within. The roof was found to have dropped by seven inches in one place!

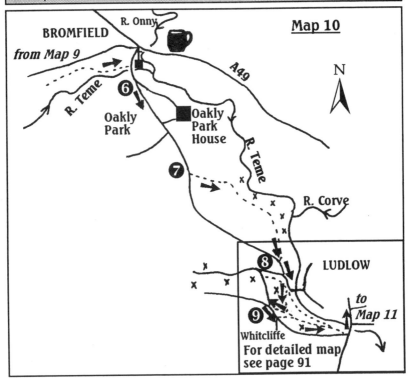

For detailed map see page 91

Leintwardine to Ludlow

Ignore a metalled track going right – this time indicated as a public bridleway, as is the main drive. The drive begins to descend and reaches a metal gate across it – usually locked and bearing a 'No Entry to Unauthorised Vehicles' sign. Walk around the gate to continue along the drive which now leaves the more formally landscaped parkland to enter wilder woodland, narrowing and becoming more of a track.

At the bottom of its descent, and bending to the right, the track crosses a small stream and begins to climb. A little over 100 yards after the stream crossing it emerges from the woodland and passes a house, on the left. It continues to climb and bears right. About 160 yards after the house (and about 50 yards before some farm buildings on the right) leave the metalled track, left, along a short track leading into a field – as indicated by a public footpath sign (SO491755). **7**

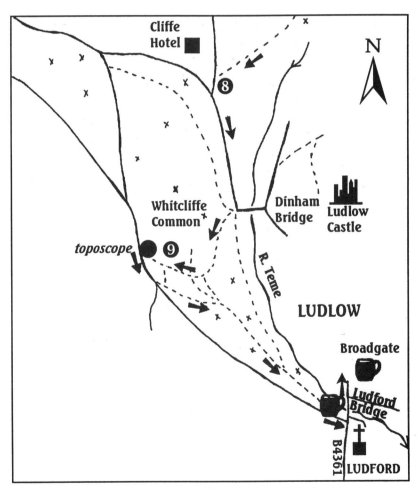

Just before leaving the metalled track look left for a good view of Titterstone Clee Hill, with Cleehill village clearly visible on its slopes to the right on a clear day.

Initially bounded by hedges, after about 40 yards the track emerges into the corner of a field. Bear half right across this.

More good views of Titterstone Clee Hill and Cleehill village while crossing the field. Part of the way across the field the tower of Ludlow church (St. Laurence) suddenly appears straight ahead.

On reaching the far (right) boundary cross a stile to the right of a gateway to enter the next field. Here maintain direction, half left from the stile and aiming well to the left of a solitary tree, to reach the far corner. Drop down to a stile and footbridge over a stream – situated just to the left of the corner of the field.

Across the stream bear slightly left up a bank to field level and then go straight ahead, towards woodland, across the field. Continue straight ahead to reach the far boundary of the field and then turn right to walk along this, the narrow strip of woodland beyond it on the left.

Towards the latter stages of the walk along the edge of this long field, and depending on time of year/tree cover, there are fleeting glimpses of the tower of Ludlow church and, more prominently, Ludlow Castle ahead.

Continue along the edge of the long field. On reaching the far corner cross a stile into the next field and bear slightly left to again follow the left hand boundary through this.

Entering the field, Ludlow Castle suddenly looms up ahead. Crossing the field, the River Teme can be glimpsed through the trees on the left.

Approaching the far side of the field the ground level drops steeply to the corner. Descend to the field corner to cross a stile, over a fence on the left. Bear immediately right to cross a stream, via a 'footbridge' which has been made by providing a fallen tree trunk with a wooden handrail. Over the stream go straight ahead to cross another stile into a field. Here follow the left hand boundary – still with woodland beyond it – with an initial steep climb to regain the height lost at the end of the previous field.

Walking along the edge of the field, the land on the left soon begins to fall away towards the river below and the boundary likewise bears away left, with breaks in the tree cover. Maintain direction along the top of the slope.

Depending on the time of year/tree cover by looking slightly behind to the left here it may be possible to see the confluence of the Rivers Teme and Corve. Good views, to the left, of both Ludlow Castle and church from the latter stages of this field crossing.

Crossing the latter stages of the field bear half right (heading to a point slightly to the left of the Cliffe Hotel which will be seen alongside a road across the field to the right) towards the far right hand corner. Here pass through a metal farm gate, to emerge onto a quiet road. Turn left along this. **❽**

Look over the first metal farm gate on the left after passing Cliff Park (a chalet park on the right of the road) for a good view of Ludlow Castle, St. Laurence's Church and, far in the distance to the left of these, Titterstone Clee Hill.

Remain on the road, passing Cliff Park – a chalet park – on the right. Where it joins a more significant road continue straight ahead, along a pavement which begins on the left, passing a row of old almshouses on the right.

The old almshouses are known as Clive Cottages. They were built sometime before 1811 by the Earl of Powis and restored in the 1850s in memory of his nephew, Robert Henry Clive of Oakly Park.

The roar of water hereabouts announces the presence of Dinham Weir in the river on the left. Walking out of Ludlow in the early morning I have often seen herons fishing off the weir.

Dinham Bridge was built in 1823 and replaced an eighteenth century bridge which itself had replaced a timber bridge built on stone piers, the latter probably being reused in the eighteenth century structure. The old piers can still be seen just downstream of the current bridge when the river is low. The previous bridge and castle are the subject of a well-known Turner painting of about 1790.

The part of Ludlow known as Dinham takes its name from Joce de Dinan who was granted land here in 1130 when the de Lacy family – founders of both castle and settlement at Ludlow – temporarily fell out of favour with the Crown. He also held Ludlow Castle for a time during the troubled reign of King Stephen, 1135-1154.

When the pavement reaches the parapet of Dinham Bridge cross the road to pass through a gap in the parapet wall, opposite. Here take the middle of three footpath options – a track which climbs half left. (The other two options here are a path which bears slightly right up steps and is waymarked with Mortimer Trail signs and a riverside path which goes left.) The initial section of the track has been given a stony/gravel surface.

A few yards up the track look behind for a wonderfully photogenic view of Dinham Bridge with Ludlow Castle looming up behind it.

The track climbs steadily up Whitcliffe. Initially stony it soon crosses sections of exposed bedrock and then takes on more of a dirt surface. Seats are strategically provided for those who require some respite from the climb.

A more level section provides the opportunity to sample views down to the river below. Climbing again, and with a stony surface, the track bears right – around a rocky outcrop. On reaching a Y-junction go right, up some steps. At the top of the steps go straight across a narrow dirt path to climb up a grassy path, a road above to the left now making its presence known.

Ignore a path going up sharp left but instead continue straight ahead across and up a grassy area towards a seat. Gaining height, more seats appear ahead. Head towards these and a toposcope/information plinth beyond (SO506743). ❾

· *The view from the toposcope on Whitcliffe Common is the classic view over Ludlow as reproduced on countless postcards. The information plaque on its stone plinth identifies the main features which may be seen on a reasonably clear day. The town is seen laid out in the foreground with Titterstone Clee Hill dominating the view beyond.*

Half right in the distance the Bronze Age Caynham Camp hill fort is visible. Cleehill village can be seen on the middle right slopes of Titterstone Clee Hill. Further over to the right are the twin peaks of Brown Clee Hill – Abdon Burf and Clee Burf. In the foreground the town is dominated by the castle and the tower of St. Laurence's church. In the half distance, between the castle and Brown Clee Hill, is the dome of the Roman Catholic church of St. Peter's – built in 1936. Rather gruesomely the information plaque also locates Gallows Bank – a green triangle of undeveloped land half right where the gibbet formerly stood.

Whitcliffe Common was acquired by the Burgesses of Ludlow in 1241, its 'common' status allowing the grazing of livestock, gathering of hay and firewood, and the quarrying of building stone. It is now owned by the Plymouth Estates and managed, for the public benefit, by The Friends of Whitcliffe Common – successors to the former Whitcliffe Commoners Association. At 42 acres the common is only one third of its previous size – reduced in extent by minor encroachments over the years and by the sale of 78 acres in 1793 to pay for paving and lighting in Ludlow.

Still visible beside the road across the common and in the woods as the route heads down to Ludford Bridge are a number of long trenches which are thought to have been dug by Parliamentarian forces during the siege of Ludlow in the Civil War, 1646.

From the toposcope/information plinth climb up the steps to the road and turn left along it. Walk along the grass verge at its edge. After about 100 yards take a path which drops down half left from the road. (A stony track leading to a public car park leaves the right hand side of the road at the same point.)

Within a few yards, by a seat, ignore a path going off and down sharp left but maintain direction. The path here is just above and to the right of the route up to the viewpoint. It passes through open woodland descending steadily. At a clearing the path merges with two others, coming in from the left, and becomes wider. Remain on it, maintaining direction and descending along the edge of Whitcliffe, the road about 100 yards to the right through the trees. Still descending the obvious path takes on a stony/gravel surface.

The noise of various rapids in the river – below left – can be heard. Ludlow takes its name from these – 'Ludelaue', meaning 'the hill/mound beside the loud waters'.

Ignore a path going off sharp left down to the river (the other end of the riverside path ignored at Dinham Bridge), but continue straight ahead. A level section of path follows.

Depending on the time of year/tree cover there are good views to be had across the town, to the left. The path here is right on the edge of Whitcliffe, as evidenced by a number of 'Danger. Sheer Drop' signs hereabouts.

The path – quite wide and with a good stony surface – begins to descend steeply and eventually reaches the road, down a flight of steps. Go straight ahead along the pavement from the bottom of the steps to reach a T-junction with the B4361 road. Here turn left to reach Ludford Bridge, passing the Charlton Arms public house *en route*.

Ludford Bridge, over the River Teme, is a fifteenth century structure although its foundations may be much older. There was formerly a chapel on it – St. Catherine's – which in 1406 was occupied by a hermit, Thomas Shelve of Leintwardine. There are wonderful views of the river to be had from the bridge but any sense of tranquillity is soon shattered by traffic on the busy B4361 which crosses it.

The River Teme here originally formed the boundary between Shropshire and Herefordshire, with Ludford being in the latter county. Both it and neighbouring Ludlow are now in Shropshire however.

Ludford is a much older settlement than its neighbour and is mentioned in Domesday Book, 1086. The small settlement here is often overlooked by the visitors rushing into Ludlow but has much of interest.

At the T-junction with the B4361 look right to see a large building with four chimney stacks – the service range of Ludford House, probably sixteenth century in origin. The chimneys may be a legacy from a previous building on the site, the Leper Hospital of St. Giles.

Just around the corner to the left at the T-junction is a wonderfully eccentric pair of dwellings – Cliff Villas – with mock-Tudor windows and a black-and-white upper storey. They date from 1841 and were erected by Edmund Lechmere Charlton, squire of Ludford. Charlton is reputed to have fought the last duel held in England. The Charlton Arms public house lies just beyond Cliff Villas, overlooking Ludford Bridge and the river.

Over Ludford Bridge the building on the right which faces Ludford across the river and has the large gothic arch included in its fabric is St. John's House, the site of the former St. John's Hospital which was purchased by William Foxe after the dissolution of the monasteries and used as his residence, being remodelled as such in 1540. It was founded in the thirteenth century to care for the sick and poverty-stricken but later became more of a quasi-religious establishment. The surviving and much restored gothic arch was possibly the south entrance to its nave.

Sixteenth century brass of Jane Foxe in Ludford church

Cross Ludford Bridge – with care, there is no pavement and the road is very busy – and walk up Lower Broad Street, straight ahead, to Broad Gate where this stage of the walk ends.

Broad Gate is the only survivor of seven gates through Ludlow's town walls. It originally possessed a portcullis. The original medieval gate is largely hidden by sixteenth, seventeenth and eighteenth century domestic architecture but can be better appreciated from underneath, with the groove for the portcullis visible. The cellars of the adjacent Wheatsheaf public house contain the remains of the supports for the drawbridge which formerly spanned the defensive town ditch outside the gate.

The Wheatsheaf public house, to the right of Broad Gate, was built between 1664 and 1668 in the old town ditch and on the site of a building destroyed at the time of the siege of Ludlow, 1646, during the Civil War.

Ludford Church

The tower of Ludford church – St. Giles – is visible slightly right ahead from the T-junction with the B4361. To visit the church turn left onto the B4361 and then right, off it, opposite the Charlton Arms, into a quiet lane. Then bear right through ornate metal gates to walk up the churchyard path which bends to the right, a row of old almshouses down to the left.

There has been a church on this site since the twelfth century at least – a Norman window from that period survives in the west wall of the nave – but until the dissolution of the monasteries under Henry VIII Ludford was only a chapelry, subservient to the Benedictine Priory at Bromfield, passed earlier on this stage of the walk.

The nave of the church is twelfth century (but was so heavily restored in 1866 that it should properly be considered to be Victorian), the chancel dates from about 1300, and the tower is fourteenth century in origin. The large chapel on the north side of the church (the Foxe Aisle), was added by William Foxe in the sixteenth century and contains brasses of him and his wife, Jane. These depict Foxe, who died in 1554, in armour somewhat old-fashioned even for this date. The chapel contains other tombs of both the Foxe and Charlton families. The tomb of Sir Job Charlton, in its south-west corner, is particularly impressive – with the recumbent effigy of the baronet dressed in his judicial robes. He died in 1697.

Ludford House

Ludford House to the west of the church was originally built in the late sixteenth century by William Foxe, although the house has had a long and complicated architectural history since then. Foxe was a member of a successful legal family and had twice represented the borough of Ludlow in Parliament. After the dissolution of the monasteries under Henry VIII he purchased St. John's Hospital, just across the river in Ludlow, where he then lived, as Lord of the Manor of Ludford. It is thought that he originally built the mansion in Ludford for his son Edmund who was unfortunately to die before him.

The Foxe family did very well out of the dissolution of the monasteries for it was another son, Charles, who was to purchase the Priory at Bromfield. It was William Foxe who first built almshouses on the site below Ludford church although the buildings now seen on the site were erected by a later resident of Ludford House, Sir Job Charlton, in 1672. They have since been known as Sir Job Charlton's Hospital.

The Manor of Ludford passed from the Foxe family to the Charlton family in 1637, sold for £500 to meet debts. It was not to change hands again until 1920. Job Charlton, who lived at Ludford from 1637 until his death in 1697 was one of the most distinguished judges of his day. He was Speaker of the House of Commons for a time. The importance of the Charltons locally is celebrated in the name of the public house which overlooks Ludford Bridge – the Charlton Arms.

Ludlow

Whilst neighbouring Ludford is mentioned in *Domesday Book* (1086) Ludlow is not and it is not until 1138 that it is first recorded as a place name. The name itself is derived from 'Ludelaue' meaning a hill or mound beside loud waters, i.e. rapids.

Ludlow is very much a medieval planned town, begun under the de Lacy family – supporters of William the Conqueror who were given land hereabouts and began building the castle in about 1086. The town's obvious grid plan incorporates an earlier through route along the present Corve Street and Old Street. It seems likely that the original crossing of the River Teme was at the bottom of Old Street. The only other distortion of the grid plan is where the existing castle was enlarged into it, at its north west corner.

Between 1233 and 1304 the town was walled. The walls were one mile around with 7 gateways through them. Only one of these, Broad Gate, still stands although many sections of the wall remain, such as that in St. John's Road which runs off Lower Broad Street by Broad Gate.

By 1377 the population of the town was 1700, making it the thirty-third largest settlement in England.

In the fourteenth century one third of the properties in the town were owned by the Palmers' Guild, a quasi-religious organisation formed in the thirteenth century and claiming links with the crusaders. The Guild invested in property and used its profits to help its less fortunate members and the town in general through the provision of almshouses and schools. It was dissolved in 1551, a late casualty of the Dissolution of the monasteries and religious orders started under Henry VIII.

Also in the early fourteenth century Ludlow Castle passed to the powerful family of Marcher Earls, the Mortimers, and thence to the House of York on the cessation of the direct Mortimer male line in 1425. In 1459, during the War of the Roses, the town was sacked after the rout of the Yorkists by Henry VI at the 'battle' of Ludford Bridge.

The town was at the zenith of its power and influence between 1534 and 1689 when it was the main seat of the Council of the Marches. Wales and the border counties were effectively ruled from the town during this period. Much building and rebuilding took place during these years – the Feathers Hotel is an example.

During the Civil War the town was besieged by Parliamentarian forces, in 1646, and many buildings outside of the town walls sustained damage. Ironically the siege seems to have seen only sporadic fighting and many of the houses destroyed at this time were in fact demolished by the Royalist defenders to deny the enemy cover. The siege itself lasted thirty-three days before the town was surrendered.

The Council of the Marches was suspended during the Civil War and was finally dissolved in 1689, the town then losing much of its former importance although it remained something of a fashionable social and cultural centre until the middle of the nineteenth century.

For a time the town was an important centre for the manufacture of gloves, the industry reaching its peak around 1700 but in decline by the early years of the nineteenth century. The major effects of the Industrial Revolution largely bypassed the town.

A railway from Shrewsbury reached Ludlow in 1852 – the Shrewsbury & Hereford Railway.

For such a small town Ludlow is rich with interesting buildings – in fact over 500 of the town's buildings are listed as being of historical interest, a higher proportion to population than any other town in the country except Bradford-on-Avon. I have included some of the more important and interesting in the 'Ludlow Town Trail' section of this book.

Stage 7

Ludlow to Richards Castle

Mileage: 6½ Miles
(From Ludlow: 4 miles to Ashford Carbonel)
O.S.Maps: 1:50000 (Landranger): 137 (Ludlow);
1:25000 (Explorer): 203 (Ludlow)

Leaving Ludlow the route initially remains near the River Teme, on quiet roads, before turning away from it to climb up onto the low ridge of Tinkers Hill. A walk along the length of this, through woodland, is followed by a stretch on a quiet road leading to the village of Ashford Carbonel, with its interesting church and water mill.

Crossing the river, the small settlement of Ashford Bowdler is visited – the church here precariously sited at the water's edge. The busy A49 is swiftly crossed and then a mixture of tracks, quiet roads and fieldpaths take the stage to its destination.

STARTING at Broad Gate, facing Lower Broad Street and Ludford Bridge, turn left to walk past the Wheatsheaf and along St. John's Road.

There is a fine surviving stretch of the old town wall of Ludlow to the left along St. John's Road.

Walk the full length of St. John's Road to a T-junction with Old Street. Go straight across Old Street to pass through an archway into Friars Walk.

A pleasant backwater of Ludlow, Friars Walk is part of a very ancient trackway from Clee Hills which follows the line of the walls to the south of the town – along what are now St. John's Road, Silkmill Lane and Camp Lane. It takes its modern name from the fact that there was an Augustinian Friary just south of, and adjacent to, its route here.

The friars arrived in the town in 1254 and settled initially in Christ Croft – one of the original grid plan streets in the Dinham area of the town which has long since disappeared. In 1256 the friars moved to the site at Lower Galdeford and were so successful there that by 1284 what is now Friars Walk was diverted to allow expansion of the Friary. That diversion is evidenced on the ground today by the sudden bend near the end of the Walk. The Friary buildings and its fishponds were to the south (right) and its gardens to the north (left) of Friars Walk.

Walk the length of Friars Walk and on reaching a road turn right down it, passing the town telephone exchange and Severn Trent's

Ludlow depot. Just beyond a car park, on the right, turn right into Weeping Cross Lane.

In medieval times there were two crosses in Weeping Cross Lane – that of St Kellem at this end of the road and the weeping Cross at the far end, near the river. Both have long since disappeared.

Walk down Weeping Cross Lane, crossing it to use the pavement on its left-hand side. Where the road bends right, by an old toll house, turn left off it along another road. **❶**

The toll house is an early nineteenth century building. The blank window above the door probably contained the toll board.

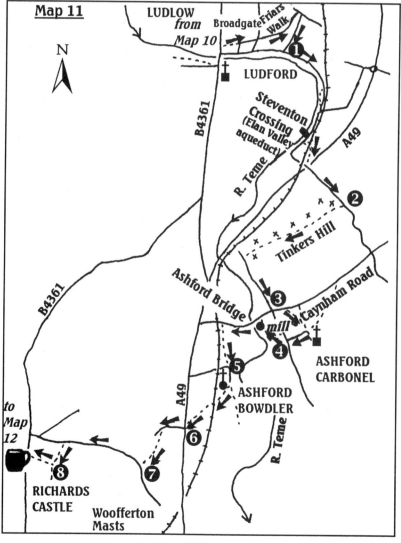

Walk along the road using the pavement on its left-hand side. The river is just to the right of the road which, after about 250 yards, passes a large building on the right – Temeside Mill.

A large cream-painted building, in stone and brick and with cast iron window frames, Temeside Mill dates from the nineteenth century. Known as the New Mill until the 1880s, corn milling ceased here at the turn of the century but in 1921 the premises reopened as the Temeside Case Mill where cases for cutlery and jewellery were made. This enterprise only lasted a decade and since then the building has variously turned out false teeth and wood-burning stoves. It is still commercially active.

Continue along the road past a Severn Trent depot, on the right. About 300 yards after this cross the road and leave it, right, over a stile to the right of a wooden gate and proceed along a riverbank path. There is a public footpath sign where the path leaves the road. Follow the riverside path, the rear gardens of houses beyond hedge boundaries on the left.

Look ahead downstream here to see the Elan Valley Aqueduct crossing the River Teme via Steventon Bridge.

On reaching a fence, and gate, across the riverside path ahead bear left to climb up a steep flight of stone steps. These emerge onto a road. Turn right along it. After about 50 yards ignore a road going left at a junction but continue straight ahead, signposted 'Ashford Carbonel 1¾ Miles'. The road begins to descend and bends left. Railway lines appear across the field to the left – the Manchester to South Wales main line. Steventon Cottage, on the right, is passed.

Steventon Cottage is a walkman's cottage for the Elan Valley Aqueduct. A water company employee responsible for overseeing a section of the aqueduct would live here and the building contains meters to monitor the water flow in the pipelines below. The end of the Steventon Bridge aqueduct crossing of the Teme, seen earlier from the riverside path, can just about be made out in the far right-hand corner of the garden of the house.

Continue on the road. About 100 yards beyond Steventon Cottage – and part of the way along a short 'avenue' section between trees – leave the road, left, over a stile and onto a footpath which runs between wire fences towards the railway lines (SO523736).

On reaching the railway lines cross a stile and then the rails – with care, it is a very busy route for both passenger and freight traffic! Entering a field, over another stile, turn right to follow the boundary with the railway lines – the busy A49 road across the field to the left. On reaching a wooden fence at the end of the field bear left to walk alongside it and to drop down to a metal farm gate, a stile alongside to its left. Cross the stile to gain access to a quiet road and turn left along this, soon crossing the A49 over a bridge.

Continue on the road which soon begins to climb. After a couple of hundred yards a level section of road precedes a second climb, woodland now commencing on the right of the road (Tinkershill Wood).

Views of Titterstone Clee Hill, to the left, from the road. Ahead left the ridge now being climbed can be seen as it continues around towards the Bronze Age hill fort of Caynham Camp.

About 40 yards before the top of the climb on the road leave it, sharp right, through a metal gate (may be open) onto a track (SO528728). ❷

The track enters the woods but then climbs and bears left to emerge from the trees, with a field on its left. On reaching a metal farm gate pass through it to enter the field and then follow its right boundary, soon passing through an incomplete boundary into another field ahead. Here again follow the right-hand boundary, woodland beyond it.

Good views behind across the top of Caynham Camp to Titterstone Clee Hill in the background.

On reaching the far corner of the field cross a fence/stile and continue straight ahead on a path through what was an area of new tree planting at the time of writing. Continue through this to reach an area of more mature trees. At the end of this short section the path runs along the top of the now much narrower ridge, outside the boundary of a field on the left and just within the woodland (right). (*Note: At the end of the section of mature trees, on reaching the field the path rounds the corner of it to proceed along the OUTSIDE of its boundary, through the very edge of the woodland. There is another path which goes straight ahead over a fence/stile here to proceed along the right-hand boundary of this and succeeding fields – parallel to the path taken – but this is not the right of way and should not be used.*)

Continue to follow the path along the top of the ridge, a hedgerow separating it from the field on the left.

Views ahead to the left here, where the hedgerow allows. Half-left are the prominent radio masts near Woofferton while beyond and further left the low hills are those behind Brimfield, including Brimfield Hill itself. To the right the woodland means that views are harder to come by but where tree cover does allow it there are good distant views to be had across to Ludlow – the prominent tower of St. Laurence's church about 1½ miles distant from here – and Mortimer Forest beyond. The noise of the busy A49 intrudes on what would otherwise be a tranquil ridge walk.

Continue along the narrow path – which at some points seems to have been converted to some kind of assault course (equestrian/mountain bike?). Eventually it begins to descend into the woodland on its right, a steeper section taking it to a level about halfway down the ridge. It drops down into and passes through a small disused quarry and then continues its gradual descent through the woodland to the bottom of the ridge – a field beyond the trees and fence to the right, railway lines and the A49 road beyond that.

Ignore a path going right through a small gate into the field. The main path bears left and climbs slightly to round another old quarry area (right). Another path joins from the left – (the parallel ridge-top path which comes out of a field on the left via a gate in its bottom corner). Continue straight ahead through the woods. Odd minor paths branch off the main path hereabouts. Remain on the main path throughout, keeping the boundary fence with the field on the right about 25 yards distant. (*Note: All the minor paths head in the same general direction as the main path anyway so to stray onto one or another of them is not a navigational disaster!*)

The path emerges from the woods onto a quiet lane. Turn left along this. The railway and A49 road are initially just across the field to the right but then both cross the river and become more distant, although their noise remains! Follow the lane to a crossroads – a little over half a mile. Here turn left onto a road – signposted 'Caynham 2¼, Cleehill 5½' (known as the Caynham Road and quite busy). ❸

After about 150 yards on the road, a gentle climb from the crossroads, and just before the gateway to a house on the left called 'The Old Vicarage' leave the road, right, over a stile into a field. Bear half-left across the field from the stile to reach another stile in the far boundary. Cross this into a small enclosed area, once the site of a maypole (see box on page 105) following a fence on the right through this (only about 15 yards) to reach a T-junction with a narrow path which runs outside the fence boundary of a large field ahead. Turn right along the path.

Crossing the first field after the road the masts of Woofferton are directly right.

Follow the narrow footpath which is confined between the field boundary fence on the left and a high hedge and tree boundary on the right, another field beyond this.

Good views across to Titterstone Clee Hill to the left, with Cleehill village visible on its middle slopes.

On reaching Ashford Carbonel church, to the right of the path, turn right – leaving the footpath for a quiet lane. The churchyard can also be entered here, through a gate (see box on page 106).

Walk down the metalled lane to reach a T-junction with a road, Ashford Carbonel Primary School on the corner, right. Turn right along the road. ❹

Notice the old bell on the rear wall of the school. The front of the building bears the date 1872 and two plaques – a diamond with three dog heads on one

The Ashford Carbonel Maypole

A narrow enclosed area, now a nature reserve, is so quickly crossed and apparently insignificant that it comes as something of a surprise to discover that public access to and usage of it, in 1874, resulted in legal proceedings which eventually ended up under appeal in the Court of Exchequer in London.

The narrow strip of land was at that time part of the large field ahead (Church Field), but was also where – under an agreement with the landowner dating from 1762 – the villagers of Ashford Carbonel would erect their maypole. Over the years the strip of land became an accepted recreational facility for the village throughout the year but all this was challenged by a new landowner, a Miss Hall, in 1874. A local case of trespass and damage brought by her against three villagers escalated into a County Court case which went in favour of the villagers as regards permanent access to the field, as did the subsequent appeal hearing in London in November 1875. Known as the Maypole Field Dispute, the case was celebrated in *Punch* with a poem entitled *The Law and the Lady of the Manor, or The Menaced Maypole of Ashford Carbonell* which begins:

'The Men of Ashford Carbonell they doughtily declared
That where their Maypole had been raised, that pole should still be reared;
But the Lady of the Manor and her myrmidons of Law
Took counsel with a view to strike those villagers with awe.
Is it in England's favoured land, on turf by Britons trod,
Where 'proputty's' a fetish, and the landlord as a god,
That resistance to the sacred rights of owners of the soil
Is found among its rustics and its humble sons of toil?'

and concludes:

'O Lady of the Manor fair of Ashford Carbonell,
Though you lose that longed-for acre, and pay legal costs as well,
What think you is the usufruct of one of many fields
To the pleasure which the village-green to landless hundreds yields?
Madam, when next that Maypole's reared in its accustomed place,
To play the Lady Bountiful, with a British Matron's grace,
Were worthier of your Sex and State than waging stubborn fight
With a plucky Shropshire parish for a more than doubtful right.'

Ironically within a few years of this outpouring of patriotic fervour the practice of erecting a maypole on the site had ceased and the fenced off school nature reserve is all that remains on the ground to recall the affair.

Ashford Carbonel Church

The church of St. Mary Magdelene, Ashford Carbonel, is sited above the village in a roughly circular churchyard which suggests a religious site of far greater age than the current, mainly Norman, building – a fact reinforced by the presence there of five ancient yew trees, two of which have a girth of some thirty feet and have been estimated as being 1500 years of age.

About half of the chancel and two-thirds of the nave are early Norman. The chancel was doubled in size in about 1200 and the western third of the nave was added about 100 years after that.

The oldest objects inside the church are a decorated stone tomb slab situated in the floor to the left of the altar – dating from the late fourteenth century – and the basin of the font which is twelfth century in origin (the base and stem date from 1883). A window next to the pulpit contains fifteenth century stained glass at its top – a decorative rose at its centre – while on its sill is a delightful little piscina.

The chancel roof was renewed during the restoration of the church in 1883 but that in the nave dates from 1600. The pyramidal roofed timber belfry dates from the mid fifteenth century. It houses three bells, two of which date from around 1320.

Just inside the door, on the right, are two early views of the church, both water-colours, the one dating from 1791 and the other from between 1820 and 1840. Outside, the Priest's Door in the south wall of the chancel dates from the second half of the eleventh century while a blocked doorway to the nave on the north side of the church dates from about 1210. At the west end of the church the surround of the lancet window bears the carvings of two stone heads – the church's only medieval sculpture.

There are several gravestones of interest in the churchyard. By the south door there is a group dating from the mid to late eighteenth century – the oldest decipherable one I could find after a very brief search was dated 1769. Near the north-east corner of the graveyard, just to the right from the entrance gate from the footpath, is an 1882 gravestone bearing the lines:

'A sudden shock – I in a moment fell;
I had not time to bid my friends farewell.
Beware! Death happens unto all;
This day I fell – tomorrow you may fall.'

It commemorates a Mrs. Lancett who was struck and killed by a train on the line just south of Ludlow while picking up nuts.

Another unusual grave is that of Arabella Yate, situated across the graveyard in its south-east corner. Its marker is a rare cast-iron tomb cover dating from 1806.

and a stag on a shield on the other (the coats of arms of the Downes and the Hall families – local Lords of the Manors).

After about 60 yards on the road leave it, left, over a stile – situated to the right of a wooden farm gate – into a field. Follow the left hand boundary of the field to its far corner and then turn right to follow the far boundary along to the next corner, the river below on the left. (Note: The public footpath sign at the stile from the road points half-right from the stile to the opposite corner of the field, which is in fact the corner now reached. While Explorer Map 203 does show a path running diagonally across the field the right of way is indicated along the field boundaries, as above.)

On reaching the corner of the field cross a stile to drop down into an orchard area. Go straight ahead through this, under apple trees.

Ashford Carbonel

The village of Ashford Carbonel takes its name from the Norman Carbonel (Carbonell) family, members of who came to England as part of William the Conqueror's invasion force in 1066. Ashford comes from the old name of the manor which was Esseford and refers to a ford across the River Teme, near ash trees.

The ford was somewhat downstream of the current bridge and is thought to have been situated on an ancient trackway from the Midlands to Wales, possibly a salt-way. Over the ford from Ashford Carbonel is Ashford Bowdler, visited later on this stage.

At the time of *Domesday Book* (1086) the manor of Esseford was held by Osbern Fitz Richard of Richards Castle. Sometime between 1174 and 1185 Osbern Fitzhugh, his son, granted the manors of 'Hesford and Huvertune' (Ashford and Overton) to William Carbonel and his heirs in return for ongoing services under arms.

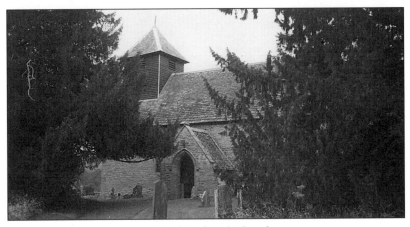

Ashford Carbonel Church

Ashford Mill and its semicircular weir will be seen half-left ahead. Remain well to the right of the building while crossing the orchard (small footpath marker posts show the way). On reaching a track to the mill turn right along it to reach a metal farm gate with a stile situated just to its left. Cross the stile to emerge onto a road and turn left along this (the Caynham Road again).

The mill was built in about 1819. Technically still capable of operating it is no longer used to grind corn for human consumption because of health

Mill Wheel at Ashford Carbonel

regulations. At the time of my first visit, in October 1999, it had been damaged by floods and was not working.

I spent a pleasant hour here talking with a gentleman of the village who was picking apples in the orchard and insisted I took samples of each of the many local varieties there with me to try later. Without exception they were delicious and a far cry from the tasteless offerings on sale in most shops today! While we talked about the village, the mill and the apples we watched a goldcrest performing acrobatics in the apple trees.

The road swings left to cross the Teme via Ashford Bridge.

Designed by Thomas Telford and built in 1797 at a cost of £830 the single span brick bridge here was quite revolutionary in its day in that Telford decided to make the spandrels hollow in order to reduce weight. The bridge has a span of 81 feet. It was partially rebuilt under Thomas Groves in 1877. There is a good view of the weir to the left from the bridge.

Continue on the road over the railway bridge (see below) for a further 200 yards to reach the A49 road at Ashford Crossroads. Buses on the 731 Ludlow – Tenbury Wells route stop here in both directions of travel. The very occasional bus on this route runs into Ashford Carbonel village.

Over the river, remain on the road which makes a long bend right and climbs gently to a bridge over railway lines. Do not cross the bridge but instead leave the road, left, over a stile (at the near end of the left parapet of the bridge) and down a flight of some twenty concrete steps into a field (SO517711). Follow the right-hand boundary through the field, the railway lines beyond.

Towards its latter stages the field narrows. Ignore a footpath going right over a stile to cross the railway lines but at this point leave the boundary, bearing half-left towards a metal farm gate in the far left corner of the field. Cross a fence/stile to the right of the gate and proceed straight ahead along a green lane/track which in less than 50 yards emerges onto a road at a bend, a level crossing over the railway lines a little way to the right. Turn left along the road – actually straight ahead from the green lane – to pass through the small settlement of Ashford Bowdler. ❺

Turn right on reaching the road at Ashford Bowdler, cross the railway at the level crossing and continue along the road for about 350 yards in total to reach the A49 road at Ashford Bowdler Turn. Buses on the 731 Ludlow – Tenbury Wells route stop here in both directions of travel.

At a Y-junction bear right. (The junction is formed by the drive to the church leaving the road, left, through a gate which is usually open. Bear left to visit the church. If visiting the church bear to the right of the vicarage to rejoin the road rather than returning down its drive.) The road ends in front of two dwellings. Continue between these to reach a wooden farm gate into field, a stile alongside it (SO518705). There is an old metal wind pump in the field.

The radio masts at Woofferton are half-right in the distance across the field. Crossing the field, the spire of Ashford Bowdler church is directly behind,

Cross the stile into the field and bear right/half-right, towards railway lines beyond its boundary. On reaching the boundary cross a stile and then the railway lines – with care, it is the same busy route crossed earlier in the day. Over the railway cross another stile into a field.

Follow the left-hand boundary across this field, after a few yards crossing a depression in the ground which may contain water after wet weather. Reaching the corner of the field, in the absence of a stile either pass through, or climb over, a farm gate which is situated about 10 yards in from the field corner. Bear half-left from the gate, across a farm track, to enter the corner of an adjacent field – again either through or over the gate. (*Navigation Note: Head directly towards the distant Woofferton masts here.*) Maintain direction through this field, heading towards its far corner, the busy A49 road beyond.

Ashford Bowdler

Ashford Bowdler stands on the other side of the old ford across the River Teme from Ashford Carbonel. The Bowdler part of its name seems to have come from the de Boulers family, Norman tenants hereabouts.

The church (St. Andrew's), is thought to have been founded around 1211 or slightly earlier, possibly by Henry de Boulers, on land owned by the Priory at Bromfield – passed on Stage 6 of the walk. The church stands right on the banks of the Teme – a picturesque setting but one which has caused misfortune down the years, with the entire east end of the chancel, including its pulpit and old wooden furniture, collapsing into the water in 1905.

The building is essentially Norman in origin. There are two blocked Norman doorways, one on each side of the nave, while the extant entrance probably dates from the fifteenth century. (The blocked doorways may have been used by pilgrims/travellers passing through the building and seeking a blessing from the priest *en route*.) The church is surmounted by an oak shingled spire. The churchyard contains a number of fine eighteenth century headstones, a guide to which is available in the church.

Approaching the church, along its entrance drive, on reaching a point level with the large vicarage (which is on the right), look behind for a distant sighting of the church tower of St. Laurence at Ludlow.

In the corner of the field a stile gives access onto the A49. Turn left along the road, remaining on the left-hand side of it to benefit from the wide grass verge. ❻

On reaching the road turn around for a good view of the spire of Ashford Bowdler church with Titterstone Clee Hill in the distance beyond. The ridge of Tinkers Hill, walked earlier on the stage, is half-left.

The short walk along the busy A49 leaves one in no doubt as to the preferred means of travel. 'Racetrack' does not begin to describe it!

After about 175 yards on the road cross it – *with extreme caution* – to take a track going right off it (SO515701). The stony/partly metalled track climbs steadily from the road. As the climb finishes it passes through a metal farm gate and over a cattle grid and bears left – heading directly towards the Woofferton masts. About 55 yards after the cattle grid a hedge which has been on the left of the track ends to be replaced by a fence which veers away left from the track. About 10 yards after the hedge ends leave the metalled track, half-left, on an indistinct grassy track which initially parallels the course of the wire fence on the left and soon runs immediately alongside it. The Woofferton masts are still directly ahead while ahead and slightly to the right, on the metalled track just vacated, are the buildings of Featherknowl Farm.

Just before reaching a metal farm gate adjacent to the nearest of these buildings cross a stile over the fence on the left. Turn right to continue in the same general direction through the adjacent field, following the boundary which is now on the right.

Follow the right-hand boundary through the field – an orchard beyond the boundary hedge once the buildings of Featherknowl Farm have been left behind. On reaching the corner of the field pass through a metal farm gate onto a track. (There is a stile about 10 yards to the left of the farm gate but at the time of writing it was so overgrown as to be impassable.)

Go straight ahead across the metalled farm track and through the field beyond. Nearing the bottom of it head towards where the corner of an adjacent field juts out into it on the left. At that corner cross two stiles into the adjacent field and maintain direction through this, the boundary with the field just vacated on the immediate right. On reaching the far boundary of the field cross a stile, situated just to the left of an oak tree, to emerge onto a quiet road (SO509695). Turn right along the road. ❼

(Note: If the field after the metalled farm track is in crop, as it has been on the occasions I have passed this way, then an easier option is to turn right along the track and on reaching a 'crossroads' of tracks turn left. Continue along this track to reach the quiet road – about 140 yards further along it than where the footpath reaches it – and turn right along this.)

Crossing the fields, the spire of Orleton church is directly ahead – about two miles distant – while over to the left the church with the large square tower and red roof is at Batchcott – (an 1892 replacement for the old church in the hills at Richards Castle) – about 1¼ miles away.

At the start of the road walking Batchcott church is directly ahead while on a clear day those with keen eyesight may just be able to spot the old church in the hills at Richards Castle which is visited early on Stage 8. Look half-left ahead.

Walk along the quiet road. The radio masts at Woofferton are initially to the left but gradually fall behind. The road meanders along but overall bears gradually left. It passes the entrance drive to a large concentration of farm buildings and then the isolated Brick-kiln Cottage,(marked as Brickyard Cottage on Explorer Map 203) – both on its right.

By now the church in the hills above Richards Castle is directly ahead in the hills.

The road meanders on and starts to climb gradually.

As the road begins to climb turn around and look half-left over the hedge for a superb and unexpected view behind which includes Tinkers Hill and Caynham Camp, in the middle distance, with Titterstone Clee Hill beyond them.

Eventually, after a little over three quarters of a mile on the road and just before it bends right to a steeper section, leave it for a footpath which goes left through a metal farm gate into a field – as indicated by a public footpath signpost (SO498697). Follow the initially straight right-hand boundary of the field. Where a stream in that boundary causes it to bend out into the field walk around that bend and then bear right to cross the boundary and stream via a footbridge. (Note: This footbridge can be difficult to locate in late summer when it may be overgrown.) ❽

At the footbridge the route leaves Shropshire to re-enter Herefordshire. Walking here one October afternoon I surprised a fox.

Across the wooden footbridge, bear slightly right to follow the right-hand boundary across the next field. On reaching the far corner pass through a small wooden gate into the next field, the houses of Richards Castle appearing ahead at the top of it. Again follow the right-hand boundary up this field, passing just to the right of a tennis court. On reaching the top right-hand corner of the field cross a stile into a small paddock/orchard area. Continue straight ahead across this, a gradual climb like the field before it, to reach a stile in its far (top) boundary. Cross this to reach the B4361 road. (Take care, there is not much of a verge here!)

Turn right along the road. After only about 30 yards cross it to reach the Castle Inn, on the left, where this stage of the walk ends.

 Bus stops for both direction of travel on the 192/292 Birmingham – Ludlow – Hereford route are a few yards further along the road from the Castle Inn. Further still along the road on the left is a telephone box.

The Castle Inn bears one of the old round Automobile Association signs – Ludlow 3½ miles, Leominster 7, and London 138½.

Stage 8

Richards Castle to Aymestrey

> Mileage: 8 Miles (from Richards Castle: 3 miles to Orleton
> Common)
> O.S.Maps: 1:50000 (Landranger): 137 (Ludlow);
> 1:25000 (Explorer): 203 (Ludlow)

*Leaving the B4361 and modern site of Richards Castle the route climbs,
via fieldpath and minor road, to visit the old church and castle in a fold of
the hills above. There then follows a circuitous route to the scattered
settlement of Orleton Common, mainly over tracks and quiet roads.*

*A long gradual climb up to Bircher Common – more quiet roads but
mainly tracks – is followed by a section through woodland (Croft Woods)
and a spectacular walk along the ridge below the hill fort at Croft Ambrey.
There are superb views across the Vale of Wigmore and beyond to be had
from the viewpoint at the north-west corner of this.*

*A direct and rapid descent from the hill fort takes the route through the
small settlement of Yatton from where tracks and a short final section of
road bring it to the banks of the River Lugg at Aymestrey, the end of the
stage and of the Riversides Way.*

STARTING at the Castle Inn turn right along the B4361 road. After
about 100 yards, at the top of an initial rise, turn right along a stony
track – passing between cottages. Continue on this track until it
makes a 90-degree bend to the left, a white house on the corner. Here
maintain the original direction of the track by leaving it, right, over a
stile into a field.

Follow the right-hand boundary up the field. Initially that boundary
is that with the back gardens of a row of dwellings on the right but
further up the field a hedge replaces them. On reaching the top
right-hand corner of the field cross a stile, situated just to the right of a
metal farm gate. Emerging onto a track go straight across it and over
another stile into the field ahead (SO491696). **❶**

Go straight ahead across the field from the stile to locate another stile
in its far boundary. Cross this, a wooden footbridge beyond it and a
further stile to enter the next field. The footbridge crosses a small
seasonal watercourse.

*Crossing the field before the footbridge, look almost straight ahead for an
initial view of the church of St. Bartholomew, Richards Castle, on its hill top
setting, the mound of the castle alongside it.*

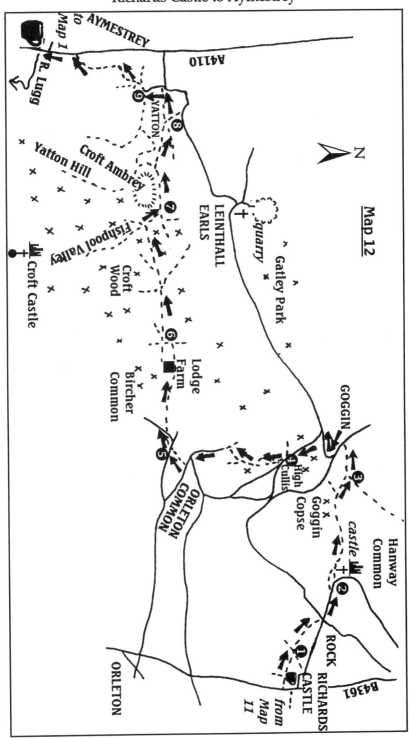

Map 12

N

to AYMESTREY

Map 1

R. Lugg

A4110

YATTON

⑨

⑧

Croft Ambrey

Yatton Hill

Fishpool Valley

Croft Wood

Croft Castle

⑦

⑥

LEINTHALL EARLS

quarry

Gatley Park

Lodge Farm

Bircher Common

⑤

GOGGIN

High Cullis

Goggin Copse

④

③

ORLETON COMMON

castle

Hanway Common

②

ROCK CASTLE

RICHARDS CASTLE

①

from Map 11

B4361

ORLETON

Entering the next field bear half-left towards its far left corner to locate a stile which is situated immediately to the left of a stream which runs along the field boundary. Cross the stile onto a muddy track and go straight across this to cross another stile into a small paddock beyond. The buildings of Lower House Farm will be seen along the track to the right. Go straight ahead from the stile up the paddock, keeping its right-hand boundary (and stream) about 10 yards distant. *(Note: When I was last here there seemed to be a barn under construction in the paddock to the immediate left of the footpath. Whether or not this will affect the routing of the path remains to be seen.)*

Cross a stile in the top boundary of the paddock into the next field. Again go straight ahead up this. On reaching a stony track bear right along it to a metal farm gate. Passing through this remain on the track which soon reaches a T-junction with a quiet road (SO482700). Turn right along this and on reaching a crossroads (Rock, on Explorer Map 203) go left, signposted for Hanway.

Green Farm – on the left of the road as it climbs – dates from 1561 when it was the manor house of Richards Castle. It was built by John Bradshaw who was renting the manor at that time. The farm takes its current name from its proximity to the village green of the old settlement. In 1652 it was bought by Major Richard Salwey and the family have owned it ever since.

The road climbs steeply from the crossroads. Remain on it as it passes the large building of Green Farm – on the left – but just after this leave the road, half-left, up a stony track. The track initially parallels the road but then bears left to pass to the left of a small green with an oak tree on it and a cottage beyond (Old Church Cottage). Continuing to bear left the track reaches the green gates of St. Bartholomew's church – on the right. ❷

Go through the gates and up the short stony path beyond to visit church and castle (see boxes on pages 117 and 118) or remain on the track to continue with the walk.

(Having visited the church and castle ruins return down the path and through the green gates and then turn right along the track – a public bridleway.)

Beyond the gates to the church the track becomes grassy. Almost immediately it passes through a metal gate into a field, becoming less distinct. Go straight ahead from the gate towards another metal gate in the opposite boundary. Pass through this onto a stony track and turn right along it (SO484702).

The stony track initially has coniferous woodland to its left and the tree covered castle mound above it on the right. It passes through a metal farm gate (may be open), a pond down to its left, and begins a gradual descent. At the end of a left bend it reaches a ford – a stream running along it for about 15 yards. Remain on the track – there is a footbridge on its left across the stream – which begins to climb beyond the ford. Ignore a dirt track going off and up sharp left. The stony track continues its gradual climb – a fence to its right, open hillside to the left and ahead (left) a conifer plantation.

Below the conifer plantation, the track passes through another metal farm gate – its surface now a lot less stony. Remain on it as it continues to climb along and below mixed woodland, on the left – Goggin Copse. Now more of a grassy track, and deeply rutted in parts, it climbs more steeply towards the boundary of this woodland. On reaching the corner

St. Bartholomew's Church

Little used today, the Norman church of St. Bartholomew is beautifully sited in the hills above the modern village. It was probably founded by Richard Fitz Scrob, a Norman noble who had come to England some years before the Conquest of 1066 in order to serve Edward the Confessor.

The church possesses a detached early fourteenth century tower to its east. It was probably sited here for reasons of defence as regards the adjacent castle. If west of the church, it could have been used by attackers to besiege the castle. Significantly all its windows face north, south or east and so cover any area of attack the castle could not. The tower contains three bells, the oldest dating from early in the sixteenth century.

The church itself is entered through a fifteenth century porch. Inside, the nave is Norman and has two surviving windows from this period in its north wall. Most of the remainder of the building dates from the fourteenth century. In the nave, resting against the wall just to the left of the entrance, is a thirteenth century carved stone coffin lid. The carving is of a foliated cross. Nearby is an ancient font bowl.

In the south wall of the chancel is a walled up, part-buried arched doorway and window. These belong to a crypt or hermit's cell known as St. Anthony's Bower – after a fourth century hermit of that name.

The north transept of the church – St. John's Chapel – dates from about 1351 and was a chapel of the Knights Templars, founded by Hugh Mortimer. It contains an old canopied wooden family pew which was used by the Salwey family – who have held the Manor of Richards Castle for the past four centuries. The pew partly conceals a recess in the wall of the chapel which, it is thought, was constructed to take the coffin of Hugh Mortimer, its founder. On the opposite side, in the South Aisle, is the Chapel of St. Mary the Virgin, founded by Joan de Mortimer, daughter of Hugh. Note the large wooden screws securing the arcade of the nave to the south aisle.

The church seems to be full of wooden benches and box pews, some dating from the late seventeenth century.

of the trees it passes through a further metal farm gate, joining another track as it does so.

Entering a field through this gate the track becomes less distinct. Follow the right-hand boundary fence and hedge through the field, ignoring a footpath which goes downhill to the left after about 40 yards.

To the left, the small rounded hill in the foreground is High Cullis and the higher hills beyond are Yeld's Hill and those leading up onto Bircher Common and eventually around to Croft Ambrey.

Continue to follow the right-hand boundary through the field. On reaching the far corner pass through a metal farm gate onto a grassy track and turn left along this (SO474701). The route now joins that of the

Richards Castle

There is little to be seen of the castle on the ground today, the site being very overgrown. To reach it from the church porch bear to the left of a large yew tree and down a flight of steps. At the bottom of these bear right on a path between graves to reach a small wooden gate into the castle ruins.

Richards Castle dates from around 1050 and was founded by Richard Fitz Scrob. Given land here by Edward the Confessor he built a very early castle on the site – reputedly one of only three stone castles in England before 1066.

By the time of *Domesday Book* (1086) the castle was held by Osbern Fitz Richard, the son of Fitz Scrob, and was called Avretone (Overton) while the adjacent settlement was called Boiton. Over the years the dominance of the castle over the immediate vicinity was reflected in the manor, including the more modern settlement below, becoming known as Richards Castle.

The earliest remains on the site today are thought to date from about 1180 and are what remains of an octagonal tower keep, probably built under Hugh de Say – a direct descendant of Fitz Scrob who had changed the family name in the meantime. Hugh's granddaughter and heir, Margaret, married into the Mortimer family of Burford who then held the castle until the late fourteenth century saw it pass, via marriage, to the Talbots. In 1264 the castle was seized and held for a time by forces supporting Simon de Montfort.

The castle appears to have been little used after the early fifteenth century – when it was garrisoned against the rebellion of Owain Glyn Dwr – and by 1540 was described as being in a ruinous state.

In 1537 the manor had passed to the Crown and in 1545 Henry VIII granted it to the Earl of Warwick – grandfather of the ill-fated Lady Jane Grey. By 1548 it was being leased out and eventually passed to Major Richard Salwey, a Parliamentarian during the Civil War. The Salwey family have held the manor since.

waymarked Mortimer Trail – with one of its marker posts just to the left as the track is met. ❸

The track almost immediately bears right and begins to descend, its surface becoming more rocky and trees overhanging it to the extent that it is almost like walking through a tunnel and may be very slippery underfoot. Remain on it as it drops down to a quiet road. On reaching the road turn left down it. It descends gently to a junction. Here turn right – following the Mortimer Trail waymarks.

The road climbs steadily from the junction to its summit and then begins to descend just as steeply. At a junction turn left (Stockin Lane). This quiet road meanders along beneath mature trees of open woodland. After about 700 yards on it, ignore a stony track going off sharp right (it leads down to Stockin Farm) but remain on the road which rises ahead. After another 70 yards, at a Y-junction, ignore both road options but turn half-right down a track indicated as a bridleway (SO473692). The route leaves that of the Mortimer Trail here. ❹

The track descends gently through woodland. Ignore a track going off it sharp right (another route down to Stockin Farm) but continue straight ahead. After this the track narrows to path width. As the descent continues a stream and pond appear down to the right in the valley bottom, through the trees. Nearing the bottom ignore a path going off and up to the left, at a junction, but remain on the main path with the stream now immediately to the right in a deep cutting.

Reaching the bottom of its descent the path passes through a metal farm gate and across a grassy area with a house on the left. The house bears a plaque – 'Aprils House, 1989' .

Passing the house continue straight ahead, on what is now a grassy/dirt track, to cross the stream, here in a culvert. With the stream now on its left the track passes through a metal farm gate and, becoming stony, climbs to a T-junction with another stony track. Turn left down this. Passing a bungalow – on the right – it gains a metalled surface to become a quiet road and shortly afterwards crosses the stream again.

Follow the quiet road past the scattered dwellings of Orleton Common – passing a small former chapel (on the right) at one point and crossing the stream one final time. On reaching a road junction go right, signposted 'Orleton, Leominster'. The route of the waymarked Mortimer Trail is rejoined here and is now followed all the way to the view point at the north-west corner of Croft Ambrey.

A few yards after the road junction on the left of the road is Churn Bank Cottage which had a topiary fox (or was it a large mouse?) growing against the wall of its parking space when I last passed this way.

Topiary fox at Orleton Common

About 60 yards beyond the junction turn right off the road up a metalled track, marked 'Private Drive', as indicated by Mortimer Trail markers. This climbs to pass the large Spout House – on the left. Beyond the house the drive reaches a stony area with outbuildings/garages ahead and to the right. Continue straight ahead to take a narrow path which climbs up just to the left of the outbuildings ahead to reach a quiet road. **5**

The outbuildings/garages often seem to be home for a collection of ex-U.S. Army vehicles.

Turn right along the road. It climbs and makes a 90-degree bend left at a junction with a minor road (signed as a No Through Road). Ignore the minor road and remain on the 'main' road as it bends left and passes a house called 'Rise Hill' – on the left. Ignore a stile and gate leading up into a field on the right just after this.

About 70 yards beyond 'Rise Hill', and just after passing a second house down on the left, leave the road for a footpath which goes off right, up wooden steps and over a stile, into a field – as indicated by both a Mortimer Trail and public footpath sign (SO473677). Follow the right-hand boundary up the field – a stiff climb.

On reaching the top corner of the field cross a stile, situated to the right of a metal farm gate, into the next field. Here again follow the right-hand boundary. Nearing the top corner of this field cross a stile over a fence to the right to reach a track and then turn left up this – that is maintaining the direction of the ascent. Follow the obvious track up the hill, still fairly close to the field boundary on the right. It bears gradually right, passing well to the right of a single large ash tree, and approaches the right-hand boundary once more. The isolated buildings of Lodge Farm will be seen half-left ahead.

Richards Castle to Aymestrey

Lodge Farm, isolated and in need of some repair, can look a forbidding place on a dreary winter afternoon. I never pass it without thinking of Wuthering Heights or the Hound of the Baskervilles – but then I might have too vivid an imagination! (Stop Press! At the time of publication some repair and renovation work was, at long last, taking place, at least as regards the main farmhouse – including the replacement of its chimney stack, previously in quite alarming condition. The overall impression created by the group of farm buildings remains the same however!)

Hugging the right-hand boundary the track approaches the farm buildings and passes through a metal farm gate on the right of, and adjacent to, the first of them. Through the gate, pass to the right of the main farmhouse and, ignoring a track which drops down to the left between the outbuildings, continue straight ahead along the right-hand side of a redbrick round-roofed barn to pass through another metal farm gate.

Through this, continue straight ahead on the track which has become quite rocky underfoot since reaching the farm. Ignore a track going up to the right into a field, just beyond the gate, but continue straight ahead – the track still hugging the boundary on the right and becoming grassy and less distinct.

Beyond Lodge Farm turn and look behind for good views on a clear day. In the distance, looking just to the right of the farm buildings, the Abberley Hills will be seen – the clock tower there possibly just visible at their centre (about 20 miles distant). Half-right, the Malvern Hills rise above the far horizon (about 25 miles distant).

Cross a stile situated to the right of a wooden farm gate, after which the grassy track becomes quite sunken and narrows to path width. Follow the path up to the corner of the field – at the head of the valley – and on reaching a fence and T-junction with a grassy track turn left (SO462677). Walk along the indistinct grassy track, the fence on the right, to reach a stile adjacent to a wooden farm gate which leads out onto the open expanses of Bircher Common. **❻**

Approaching the gate and stile onto Bircher Common look left for more good views. In the middle distance are, left to right, the radio masts at Woofferton and the village of Orleton. In the far distance are the Abberley Hills and their clock tower:

Crowned by Oaker Coppice – the woodland to the far left of the route now followed – Bircher Common covers 345 acres in total.

Walk straight ahead from the stile. In just under 50 yards, at a 'crossroads' of green paths, turn right. Almost immediately, at a Y-junction of paths, again go right. Initially between bracken in season and gorse, the path soon emerges onto open grassy common and becomes less distinct.

Turn and look behind for a good view of Titterstone Clee Hill, half-left, and the distant Abberley Hills, half-right.

Continue straight ahead to cross the common, aiming to keep a boundary on the right (woodland beyond it) about 50 yards distant initially and heading towards distant woodland. *(Note: In season a better navigational guide is to keep the edge of the bracken growing at the right margin of the common on the immediate right.)* A Mortimer Trail marker post part of the way across the common will confirm the route.

Nearing the woodland ahead go straight on at a 'crossroads' of grassy paths, the path ahead now once more bounded by bracken in season. Enter the woodland via a small wooden gate situated to the left of a metal farm gate, an adjacent Forestry Commission name-sign announcing this as being Croft Wood (SO456674).

Follow the track through the wood from the gate. At a Y-junction of tracks, after about 70 yards, go right. The track meanders and undulates through the mixed, but predominantly coniferous, woodland. Eventually it makes a long, gradual bend to the right – descending as it does so. As the bend ends the descent becomes steeper. At the bottom of the slope a left bend commences. Here leave the track, right, for a path which climbs steeply up through a break in the trees. A Mortimer Trail signpost points the way (SO448669).

The arm of the Mortimer Trail signpost pointing away from the route now taken indicates a public footpath to Yarpole which goes left off the track here to drop down through the fittingly named Fishpool Valley. It passes close to Croft Castle, which may be reached from it.

The steep climb up through the tree-break can be quite slippery after wet weather and if this is the case then the best course of action is to keep well over to the left-hand side of it. A short climb, after only about 150 yards the path reaches a small wooden gate bearing a National Trust sign. Pass through this and turn left along a path, met at a T-junction immediately beyond it, now on the very edge of a steep ridge (SO447671). ❼

Croft Castle

Croft Castle lies off-route here to the south. The castle has been the home of the Croft family since the time of *Domesday Book* (1086), except for one break of 170 years – between 1746 and 1923. Cared for by the National Trust, what the visitor to it sees today is a large castellated house – a tower at each corner – with an interior basically as it was in the eighteenth century. The corner towers date from the fifteenth century.

Adjacent to the castle is the church of St. Michael which dates from the thirteenth century. A seventeenth century bell turret was painted pink when I last visited the building. Inside the church is a fine monument to Sir Richard Croft (died 1509) and his wife.

Leinthall Earls Church

The small whitewashed church of St. Andrew is almost completely hidden behind the yew trees in its ancient churchyard site but if staying in the area is very much worth a visit. The twelfth century single celled building has largely escaped the worst efforts of nineteenth century restorers. Its tremendously thick whitewashed, plastered walls are supported by crude buttresses, but that on the south side still leans alarmingly.

The building is surmounted by an octagonal wooden turret which houses a single bell. The twelfth century Norman doorway and two round-headed windows of similar age survive. Other windows in the building are simple sixteenth century additions, with the exception of the east window of about 1800. The roof is medieval and traces of ancient colouring survive on some of its timbers. Despite the proximity of the busy quarry it somehow contrives to remain an oasis of peace.

Follow the narrow path along the ridge, the hill-fort of Croft Ambrey beyond a fence to the left and a steep drop to the right. Almost immediately it passes through a wooden farm gate.

There are good views to the right all along this path to the viewpoint at the north-west corner of Croft Ambrey. The large house in woodland across the valley, just to the rear, is Gatley Park. Further behind still, those with good eyesight may just be able to make out a tall round building protruding above the trees. Shaped rather like a tall windmill this is in fact an inhabited folly in the grounds of Gatley Park. Directly opposite is the small settlement of Leinthall Earls, dwarfed by the scar of the working stone quarry behind it. The remnant of woodland above and to the left of the quarry is the strangely named Shirt and Sleeve Wood.

Croft Ambrey Hill-Fort

The Iron Age hill-fort seems to have been occupied from about 550BC and eventually covered nine acres. Excavations on the site have revealed traces of a total of 274 huts within its confines which suggests a population of around 800 by the time the Romans arrived. The main earthworks appear to date from about 390BC.

The advancing Roman legions sacked the settlement, although there is some evidence of later reoccupation and the site appears to have been used as a place of worship, or shrine, up until the second century AD.

The name Ambrey is thought to refer to Aurelius Ambrosius, a Romano-British leader who some consider to have been the subject of the King Arthur legends. However Ambrosius did not come to power until AD443 – long after Croft Ambrey was abandoned – and there is no evidence he ever visited the site.

A wonderful section of walking – but take care not to wander off the track to the right while admiring the views!

Continue to follow the narrow path along the ridge. Eventually bending left, by a group of pine trees, it reaches a seat at the north-west corner of Croft Ambrey hill-fort (SO442668).

Superb views, through 270 degrees, are to be had from this point at the north-west corner of the hill-fort. Standing on the mound near the group of pine trees facing west, on a clear day one can see:

- *Over the right shoulder: High Vinnalls (at 370 metres/1214 feet the highest point in Mortimer Forest, a fire hut at its top); Leinthall Earls, the church just visible, and the quarry behind.*

- *Half-right ahead: the whole of the Vale of Wigmore stretching northwards towards Leintwardine and beyond, to the hills behind Bucknell; Leintwardine, dominated by its church; Wigmore village, church and castle, with the wooded hills of the Wigmore Rolls (crossed on Stage 5 of the walk) above and beyond.*

- *Slightly right ahead, in the middle distance, the rounded field-covered mass of Harley's Mountain (crossed on Stage 4 of the walk).*

- *Straight ahead: in the foreground, the small settlement of Yatton; beyond that, the round wooded hill of Pyon Wood (it too has a hill-fort at its summit); beyond that, the wooded hill of Sned Wood; just to the right of this, the wooded Woodhampton Hill; in the far distance, the hills of Radnor Forest with the conical Whimble (599 metres/1965 feet in height and about 16 miles distant) prominent. Just to its right is the long, dark mass of Black Mixen (650 metres/2133 feet) with its mast, first seen on Stage 2 of the walk.*

- *Half-left: in the foreground, the first few houses of Aymestrey, Yatton Court, and the top of the church tower; beyond, the nearer of two long flat-topped hills is Mere Hill Wood while the one further over is Shobdon Hill Wood (the River Lugg flows to the right of both of these, while its gorge lies between Mere Hill Wood and Sned Wood – as walked on Stage 1).*

- *Left: in the foreground, Yatton Hill (a continuation of the hill the route is currently on); in the far distance, the northern escarpment of the Black Mountains, as far as Hay Bluff – about 22 miles distant.*

- *The route is here at a height of about 300 metres/984 feet.*

A short diversion along the path beyond the seat takes one down between the outer ramparts on the south-west side of the hill-fort.

Continuing the main route, turn right off the narrow path at the viewpoint (seat) to proceed down a wide swathe of grass, between bracken in season, which links the small group of pines with two similar groupings below. (Note: The route leaves that of the main Mortimer Trail here but continues on its waymarked Wigmore Loop for the short distance down to the isolated cottage – below.)

Just before reaching the middle group of pine trees a glance over the right shoulder behind brings a brief and unexpected view of the top of Titterstone Clee Hill.

Pass just to the left of the third group of pine trees, ignoring a sunken path which approaches from the left here before bending away again. Continue down the obvious wide grassy path, between bracken in season, the small settlement of Yatton directly ahead below. At a path 'crossroads' go straight on – as confirmed by a Mortimer Trail sign about 50 yards ahead. Just beyond this marker post the path joins a sunken track. Continue straight ahead down this towards an isolated cottage, ignoring a path which goes off to the right. The sunken track passes to the right of the cottage and through a metal gate. Here leave it, passing through or over metal barriers (fence) on the left to enter a field (SO436668). **❽**

On entering the field the low rounded mass of Pyon Wood is directly ahead beyond the small settlement of Yatton.

In the field, with the cottage on the immediate left, bear right to reach the right-hand boundary hedge and follow this down. On reaching the bottom corner continue straight ahead to climb over or pass through a wooden gate and enter the left of two fields ahead. (*Do NOT go through the gap into the right of the two fields ahead.*) Again follow the right-hand boundary of this field.

The long, flat-topped, wooded hill behind to the left is Yatton Hill which continues around from Croft Ambrey and is followed by the main route of the Mortimer Trail as it descends towards Aymestrey.

On reaching the far right-hand corner of the field pass through a metal farm gate onto a track. Proceed along this to emerge onto a quiet road. Turn left along this. The road passes through the settlement of Yatton and then bends to the left. At a Y-junction, at the start of a right bend, go right – the road losing its metalling to become a track (SO432665). The bend to the right continues. Just over 100 yards after the Y-junction, at a second Y-junction (this time of tracks) go left – the right option bears a No Through Road sign. **❾**

After about 20 yards ignore a track going left towards a field and a footpath, also left, into another field but remain on the main track which bends right and passes through a metal farm gate. Passing a modern house, on the right, it makes a major bend left and then another right to resume its original course.

Along the 100 yards or so between the two bends look to the left, slightly behind, for a good view of Croft Ambrey and the slope recently descended, with its three groups of pine trees. The long mass of Yatton Hill is directly to the left here. To the left of the track, largely hidden by new tree planting, lie the old Aymestrey sand and gravel workings.

The Aymestrey Beaker Burial

The former sand and gravel workings alongside the track from Yatton to Aymestrey were the site of an important archaeological find in 1987. Then, a hole which appeared in the ground revealed a burial site thought to date from the Early Bronze Age, between 3300 and 4000 years ago. The tomb was constructed of rough flagstones of Wenlock limestone, probably quarried from the nearby hillsides. Inside, in a crouched position, was the skeleton of a child of some seven or eight years of age. Several objects accompanied the bones, including a decorated clay pot (beaker), and a flint knife. The distinctively shaped beaker and its decoration – applied by stabbing the clay with a notched bone tool before firing – helped date the find and suggest high status. It is therefore a possibility that the Aymestrey child was the son or daughter of the head of a nearby settlement.

The Aymestrey Beaker Burial is now a major display in Leominster Folk Museum.

Continue along the stony track, which is confined between wire fences with narrow strips of new tree planting beyond. A straighter section ends with a gradual bend to the left and the track then passes a house – on the right. It takes on a metalled surface, now running alongside the garden of the house, right, and a steep wooded bank on its left. With a pond to its right it reaches the busy A4110 road.

Pass through a small wooden gate, alongside and to the right of a metal farm gate, onto the road. Turn left along it crossing it when it is safe to do so. The road is fairly busy so take care during the short walk (500 yards) along it – there is little in the way of verges on either side of it.

Ignore a road going right just before Aymestrey Bridge but continue over the bridge to reach the Riverside Inn where this stage of the walk ends.

For notes on Aymestrey and the Riverside Inn see the start of Stage 1.

A welcome at the Riverside Inn

Aymestrey

by R.Tomas

Wood smoke drifting up through trees,
Hanging in the winter chill,
Promising a welcoming;
Fires unseen, hidden until –
Reaching meadows wet from frost,
Cold again by afternoon –
We at last see lights ahead;
Curfew bell; lamps lit so soon
Day seemed hardly to have come
Before darkness closed the blinds.
River murmuring nearby,
Silent hills rear up behind –
See them menacing and black,
Stalked by our imaginings
Lurking under every tree
And each shadow's lengthening –
Hurry onwards to the glow,
As a moth drawn to a flame;
Conversations heard within,
Voices raised, then quiet again.
Ancient long house, centuries
Welcoming the traveller

The Riversides Way

To its fireside, taking in
Pilgrims who have come so far;
River flowing past its walls
Under arches worn by floods
And the passing of the years –
Turning seasons, changing moods.
Candlelight and glowing logs
Drawing men to sit awhile,
Gathered in the flickering
Light as sparks fly from the fire.
Young girl serving at the bar,
Blonde, with eyes that come alive,
Catches my smile, laughs out loud –
Twenty–something, no man's wife.
Evening passes in a glow:
Warmth and fellowship of men
Freely given, simple gifts,
Parting hope we'll meet again.
So to bed, perhaps to dream
Of the miles we've come today
The caress of eider down
Softly urging us to stay.
Crying of the owl outside
And the moaning of the trees;
Inside all is safe and still;
Sudden waking – soon at ease.
In the morning – frosty white –
Late departure, loathe to leave;
Clouds piled high upon the woods –
Can the forecast be believed?
Anything to linger here
With the girl with smiling eyes,
But the way's mapped out ahead,
And the moment's lost and flies –
Drives us onwards, calls us home –
But we promise, as we part,
To return time after time:
In this place there dwells my heart.

A Ludlow Town Trail

FOR such a small town Ludlow is rich with interesting buildings – in fact over 500 of the town's buildings are listed as being of historical importance. It would be impossible for a walking guide such as this to do full justice to all of the town's architectural treasures so I have selected some of the more significant for inclusion in this Town Trail.

The actual distance on the ground covered by the trail is about 2½ miles. The time necessary to complete it will obviously vary to the extent of coverage and as to whether the interiors of those buildings open to the public are visited. The castle alone would justify a couple of hours if fully covered. As a rough guide, however, allow 2½ hours excluding the castle.

For a short history of the town see the note at the end of Stage 6.

John Betjeman, writing in 1953, called Ludlow 'Probably the loveliest town in England' and he was by no means the first to fall under its charms. The year 1587 had found the Shrewsbury poet Thomas Churchyard waxing lyrical with the lines:

'The towne doth stand most part upon a hill,
Built well and fayre, with streates both large and wide...
And who that lists to walke the towne about,
Shall find therein some rare and pleasant things...'

What was true in 1587 is no less so today!

 Starting at Broad Gate walk down the right-hand side of Lower Broad Street.

A. Broad Gate

The only survivor of seven gates through Ludlow's town walls. It originally possessed a portcullis. The original medieval gate is largely hidden by sixteenth, seventeenth and eighteenth century domestic architecture but can be better appreciated from underneath, with the groove for the portcullis visible. The cellars of the adjacent Wheatsheaf public house contain the remains of the supports for the drawbridge which formerly spanned the defensive town ditch outside the gate.

The town was walled between 1233 and 1304. The walls measured about one mile around. There was a defensive ditch outside them. Of the seven gates through them four possessed a portcullis – Broad Gate, Corve Gate, Galdeford Gate and Old Gate – while the other three were of the postern type – Linney Gate, Mill Gate and Dinham Gate.

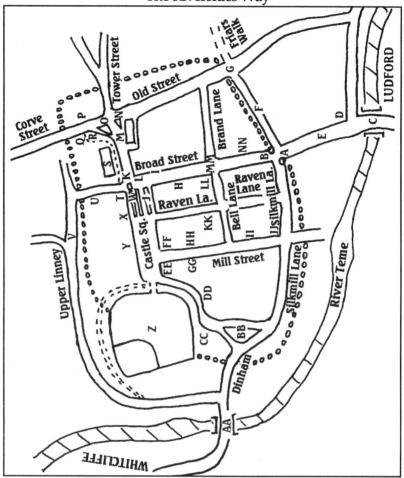

B. The Wheatsheaf

The Wheatsheaf public house, to the left of Broad Gate, was built between 1664 and 1668 in the old town ditch and on the site of a building destroyed at the time of the siege of Ludlow, 1646, during the Civil War.

 On reaching the bottom of Lower Broad Street walk out onto Ludford Bridge and turn around to look back up the street towards Broad Gate.

C. Ludford Bridge

Ludford Bridge, over the River Teme, is a fifteenth century structure although its foundations may be much older. There was formerly a chapel on it – St. Catherine's – which in 1406 was occupied by a hermit, Thomas Shelve of Leintwardine.

An older crossing of the Teme existed on the through route which pre-dated the town, at the bottom of what is now Old Street.

D. St. John's House

The building with the large Gothic arch included in its fabric is St. John's House, the site of the former St. John's Hospital which was purchased by William Foxe after the dissolution of the monasteries and used as his residence, being remodelled as such in 1540. It was founded in the thirteenth century to care for the sick and poverty-stricken but later became more of a quasi-religious establishment. The surviving and much restored Gothic arch was possibly the south entrance to its nave.

E. Lower Broad Street

Many of the buildings hereabouts were destroyed at the time of the siege of Ludlow (1646) during the Civil War.

The incline of the street was formerly much steeper until early in the nineteenth century when Thomas Telford, as Shropshire County Surveyor, lessened it by the creation of an embankment. Broad Street – beyond Broad Gate – was similarly made a cutting.

 Walk back up Lower Broad Street, on the right. On reaching the Wheatsheaf turn right into St John's Road.

F. St. John's Road

There is a good surviving stretch of the old town walls on the left along St. John's Road.

 Continue along the length of the road to reach a T-junction with Old Street.

Old Street predates the medieval grid plan of Ludlow, being part on an existing route which continues north through the town as Corve Street. There was a ford across the River Teme at the bottom of Old Street.

 Turn left to walk up Old Street passing, on the left:

G. The site of Old Gate/Lane's House (Asylum)

To the left of Lane's House is a late medieval building built onto the former town wall which may incorporate masonry from Old Gate. A metal plaque on its Old Street wall identifies the site of the gate. Lane's House itself has a black-and-white half-timbered upper storey and dates mainly from the sixteenth century. After 1676 it, together with the aforementioned medieval structure, was used as a workhouse and house of correction. In 1837 it became almshouses and was renamed Lane's Asylum

 Take the first turning on the left, into Brand Lane. Walk along this and turn right into Broad Street. Walk up the right-hand side of Broad Street, soon passing – on the left, across the road:

H. Number 53 Broad Street

The late sixteenth century frontage of this building masks a medieval open hall.

 Continuing up the street, on the right is:

I. The Angel Hotel

So called since at least 1555. The inn prospered by offering accommodation during the time of the Council of the Marches and was an important coaching inn in the eighteenth and early nineteenth centuries. In 1822 the 'Aurora' coach, with a twenty-seven hour journey time to London, departed from here. The premises contain the 'Nelson Room' wherein Lord Nelson received the freedom of the borough in 1803.

 At the top of Broad Street, with the Butter Cross ahead, take the first turning on the left into the narrow Market Street. Walk the short length of this and then, with Raven Lane on the left, turn right and then take the second turning right into the very narrow Harp Lane, to walk back towards the top of Broad Street and the Butter Cross.

J. Market Street and Harp Lane

The narrow Market Street, High Street, Harp Lane and Church Street were formed when what were originally temporary stalls in the medieval market place at the east end of what is now Castle Square were replaced by permanent buildings. There is an unusual view of the Butter Cross to be had looking along the length of Harp Lane, the narrowest of these four 'infill' streets.

 On reaching the end of Harp Lane continue straight ahead, the Butter Cross on the left and the Corner Shop on the right, into King Street.

K. The Butter Cross

This handsome building was erected between 1742 and 1744 on the site of the medieval High Cross. The architect was William Baker. The ground floor serves as a covered market; the upper has been a town hall, school and a museum in its time. It is surmounted by a wooden cupola which contains a bell thought to have come from the old chapel of St. Leonard in Corve Street.

L. The Corner Shop (Bodenhams)

A fine three-storey timber-framed early fifteenth century building, jettied on two sides. It was erected under the auspices of the Palmers' Guild in about 1404.

 Continue along King Street and through The Narrows to the Bull Ring.

M. The Bull Ring

Was known as the Beaste Market in the seventeenth century being the livestock market at that time. The Bull Ring Tavern, on the right, is another striking three-storey timber-framed building the frontage of which, like the Corner Shop (above) and many other similar buildings in the town, was for many years concealed under plaster.

 On reaching the detached building of the Tolsey, on the right-hand side of the Bull Ring, turn left down Corve Street.

N. The Tolsey

Saved from demolition under a road widening scheme in 1956, this fifteenth century building is where the market tolls were collected while its upper floor housed the market courts and administration centre.

The market courts dispensed instant justice and were known as the Court of Pie Powder – after the French 'Pieds Poudre' literally meaning the 'Dust off the Feet', i.e. justice was dished out before one had time to shake the dust off one's feet.

The detached nature of the building suggests that it was a successor to temporary market stalls.

O. The Shelde

Across the Bull Ring from the Tolsey is another small detached block of shops, again suggesting that the buildings are successors to former temporary market stalls. The row of shops was formerly called the Shelde, from the Latin 'selda' meaning stalls.

 Walk down the right-hand side of Corve Street to The Feathers Hotel.

P. The Feathers Hotel

Probably the best-known of Ludlow's timber-framed buildings, the Feathers was formerly a town house occupied by Thomas Hackluit (died 1544), Clerk to the Council of the Marches. The house was refronted and refurbished in 1619 for Rees Jones, a Welsh attorney in the Council's courts. His initials can still be seen on the surviving original door lock plate. The richly carved facade – the most exuberant of all the buildings in the town – probably dates from this time.

During the Civil War the house was used to billet Royalist soldiers. It became a public house in 1670. The balcony on the front of it was added in the nineteenth century for electioneering use.

 Cross the road to the Bull Hotel.

Q. The Bull Hotel (Inn)

The Bull Hotel is the oldest pub in Ludlow, having been carrying out that function for almost 500 years. Its frontage in Corve Street gives no clue as to the true age of the building as it was rebuilt after a fire in 1795. However, pass through to its inner yard to see its true character. The earliest record of it is as Peter the Proctor's House, in 1343, but it is thought to date back to 1199 in part. A priest hole and indoor well have been discovered within. Looking behind from its inner yard towards Corve Street the oldest timber-framed range is the jettied one to the right. It dates from late medieval times.

 Walk through to the inner yard of the Bull and continue up a flight of steps to reach the churchyard. Turn left to pass the Reader's House.

R. The Reader's House

A mid sixteenth century rebuilding of a medieval stone house once the home of Thomas Cookes (died 1513), Servitor to the ill-fated Prince Arthur. Its splendid Jacobean porch was added, in 1616, to the original stone elevation. The other side of the building is timber-framed.

In 1551 Ludlow Corporation appointed a Reader to carry out some of the duties of the Church. During the eighteenth century the Reader lived in the house.

 Beyond the Reader's House follow the narrow lane which bears right to round the parish church of St. Laurence and reach its south porch.

S. St. Laurence's Church

St. Laurence's Church dominates the whole town and is the largest parish church in Shropshire at 132 feet in height and 203 feet long. It dates from 1199 with much fifteenth century rebuilding. Rivalling many a cathedral in the quality and scale of its construction, the dominant architectural style of the church is that of mid fifteenth century Perpendicular.

Full of interest inside the undoubted highlights are the fifteenth century carved wooden misericords. Dating from around 1440 these are amongst the finest of their kind in the country.

The building also contains St. John's Chapel, the chapel of the Palmers' Guild, with its Golden Window containing a representation of St. Catherine and her wheel and Palmers' Window telling the legend of how that organisation got its charter from Edward the Confessor.

Across the church is the Lady Chapel which contains a restored fourteenth century Jesse Window. This chapel was formerly used to house the town fire engine and the wooden pegs for the fire buckets and a blocked access doorway remain.

The West window of the church depicts the Lords of Ludlow Castle ending – at bottom right – with Prince Arthur whose heart is buried somewhere in the building. He died in Ludlow Castle in 1502 while staying there with his bride of five months, Catherine of Aragon.

The superb roof dates from the middle of the fifteenth century and is the finest in Shropshire, fully reflecting the wealth and influence of the town at that time.

The entrance porch to the church is hexagonal in shape – one of only three such constructions in the country, the others being at Chipping Norton and at St. Mary's, Redcliffe, in Bristol. It is of mid fourteenth century origin.

 Leaving the church porch turn right to continue along the narrow lane. On reaching a T-junction with College Street turn right. Ahead at the T-junction are:

T. Hosyer's (Hosier's) Almshouses

Founded in the fifteenth century by John Hosyer (Hosier) – a rich draper, by the mid-eighteenth century its buildings were in a poor state of repair. The borough therefore called in the Shrewsbury architect Thomas Farnolls Pritchard – the designer of the famous Iron Bridge at Coalbrookdale – to create a new building. This, the current building, was opened in 1758. The prominent crest above its entrance is that of Ludlow borough – the white lion being that of the Mortimers and the three white roses those of the Royal House of York; the whole surmounted by the Prince of Wales Feathers.

A large plaque below the crest is in Latin but a smaller English version, just to the right of the door reads:

'The bailiffs, burgesses and community of this town of Ludlow, in the Year of Our Lord 1758, the thirty-first in the reign of the most august King

King George II, have, at their own expense, on the very foundations rebuilt, extended and decorated this almshouse originally built by the munificence of John Hosier, merchant, in the Year of Salvation 1486 and through the damage of time weakened for a long while and about to collapse. To the glory of the most good and greatest God, to the memory of the pious founder and for the more comfortable accommodation of the poor.'

The entire rebuilding cost just over £1200.

 Walk along College Street. Just beyond the church turn right, though a gateway into the churchyard – now a garden of rest.

Notice the memorial to A.E.Housman, author of the poems *A Shropshire Lad*, on the north wall of the church. Its inscription reads:

'In Memory of Alfred Edward Housman M.A. Oxon. Kennedy Professor of Latin and Fellow of Trinity College in the University of Cambridge. Author of A Shropshire Lad. Born 26 March 1859, Died 30 April 1936. Goodnight. Ensured Release Imperishable Peace: Have these for yours.'

 Return through the gate into College Street and turn right, towards the site of Linney Gate. On the left is:

U. The Rectory

This gabled building is one of the oldest in Ludlow. Its roof is fourteenth century in origin – probably between 1311 and 1328.

 Continue along College Street to reach the site of Linney Gate. Here turn left into Upper Linney.

The scant remains of Linney Gate are 'protected' by Victorian brickwork bearing a plaque which reads 'College Street 1883'.

Linney is a Saxon place name referring to the dry land above a flax growing area, where linen was produced.

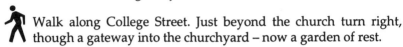 Walk the short distance along Upper Linney to reach, on the left:

V. Number 14 Upper Linney

Notice the plaque bearing the inscription 'Cooper & Bluck's Nail Manufactory 1854' on this building – a reminder that although Ludlow was mainly bypassed by the heavy industries of the Industrial Revolution there were nonetheless numerous small industrial concerns scattered around the back streets of the town, most of which have left little trace.

A Ludlow Town Trail

 Return along Upper Linney and turn right, past the site of Linney Gate, into College Street. Walk along the full length of this. At its end turn right, under an arch, into Church St

The brick 'rear' ahead at the end of College Street belongs to the Butter Cross.

The first building on the left after passing under the arch into Church Street is the rear of:

W. Tamberlaine House

Some of the carvings on the timbers of the town's buildings are works of art in themselves of which the local carpenters responsible could be justifiably proud. Some carvers left their marks to identify their work. The timbers at the rear of Tamberlaine House, in Church Street, bear such identification marks.

 Walk along the length of Church Street and continue straight ahead along the right-hand side of Castle Street/Square passing, on the right:

X. Quality Square

The buildings of this quiet backwater off Castle Street are mainly of brick and rubblestone and date from several periods. The square is entered through an arch in a sagging early brick building.

Some of the older buildings in the square were reputedly the warehouses of medieval wool merchants while there was also formerly a large, long galleried town house here, once occupied by the Foxe family. In the early nineteenth century there was a theatre in the vicinity

There is a late thirteenth or early fourteenth century window in one of the buildings behind the square. (Go into the square and to its far right-hand corner and continue through to what is now the beer garden of the Rose and Crown to locate it.) This has undoubtedly been brought from elsewhere and reset here. A likely candidate for its origin is St. Laurence's church – possibly during the fifteenth century rebuilding work there – or perhaps it is a survivor from the Foxe mansion.

Y. Number 14 Castle Street

A fine Georgian brick town house, its rainwater hoppers dated 1728. Once owned by the Baughs, a family of prominent local solicitors and clergy.

In front of the house stands Ludlow's modern war memorial – erected in September 2000 and featuring two birds (doves) atop a simple bronze shaft, itself bearing a sword and wreath, and the words 'Lest we forget'. It is the work of Walenty Pytel.

The Ludlow war memorial

In Castle Square to the left here stood, until its demolition in 1986, the Town Hall. Built in 1887 to the design of Harry Cheers of Twickenham, to replace an earlier Market Hall, the building – also known as the Corn Exchange – contained a covered market on the ground floor, and an assembly hall and Council chamber above. The architectural style, a Victorian concoction described as being 'of curly stone and virulent brick' was not to everyone's taste. Nicholas Pevsner famously described it as being 'Ludlow's bad luck'. Controversial when standing it was equally so when demolished, as the loss of a civic amenity.

The building was used for the filming of some scenes in the television drama *Blott on the Landscape.*

 Continue across Castle Square to reach the entrance to Ludlow Castle.

Z. Ludlow Castle

Ludlow Castle pre-dates the town and was built between 1086 and 1094 by Roger de Lacy, a supporter of William the Conqueror. The castle was constructed of stone from the start – quite unusual as most were wooden initially – and it is likely that the earliest part of the town grew up between it and the river around the area now called Dinham.

The castle has been much extended over the years, especially after it passed into the hands of the powerful Mortimer family, through marriage, in the early fourteenth century. When the direct male Mortimer line died out in 1425 the castle passed, via the female line and marriage, to the House of York and thence to the Crown after the Yorkist Edward IV's victory at Mortimer's Cross (1461), about eight miles to the south-west of Ludlow – a decisive moment in the Wars of the Roses. It then became a royal palace. The two sons of Edward IV – better known as 'the Princes in the Tower' stayed here for a time and it was at Ludlow Castle that Arthur, the elder son of Henry VII honeymooned with his bride Catherine of Aragon in 1501. Tragically Arthur was dead within five months – aged just 15 – and his wife went on to marry his brother, later Henry VIII. Arthur's heart is buried in St. Laurence's Church while his body was taken for burial in Worcester Cathedral. Mary Tudor, Henry VIII's daughter by Catherine of Aragon, who spent several winters at the castle, was its last royal resident.

After 1534 the castle became the main seat of the Council of the Marches – the town effectively becoming the administrative and legislative centre for Wales and the English border counties. It was a Royalist stronghold during the Civil War and was besieged by a Parliamentarian force under Colonel Birch in 1646, surrendering after 33 days.

The Council of the Marches was dissolved in 1689 and after that the castle became disused. The building was looted for building materials and soon fell into disrepair. As a 'romantic' ruin in the eighteenth century it began to attract visitors and walks were laid out around it in 1772. In 1811 it was purchased by the Earl of Powis whose descendants own it to this day.

Significant buildings within the castle grounds include:

(1) The Great Tower Gatehouse Keep – the original Norman gatehouse before the outer bailey, walls and gatehouse were built.

(2) The Chapel of St. Peter – built by Roger Mortimer in the early fourteenth century to celebrate and give thanks for his escape from the Tower of London on St. Peter's Day, 29 June 1324 – see the note under Wigmore Castle and the Mortimers at Stage 5.

(3) The Judges Lodgings – built, probably by Sir Henry Sidney before 1581, to house the many judges and court officials needed when the Council of the Marches was in session.

(4) The Chapel of St. Mary Magdalene – possibly founded under Hugh de Lacy and dating from the early years of the twelfth century, the chapel has an unusual round nave – a design which seems to have originated with the return from the Crusades of knights who had seen the church of the Holy Sepulchre in Jerusalem.

(5) The North Range – started in the thirteenth century and completed after Roger Mortimer had taken possession of the castle in 1308, this range of domestic buildings includes the Great Hall of the castle.

(6) The Garderobe Tower – built onto the outside of the Norman curtain wall of the castle in the early fourteenth century, by Roger Mortimer.

For those wishing to spend some time exploring the castle there is a very good guide book available in the shop there.

Outside the castle gate is a cannon. Russian in origin, it was captured by British forces during the Crimean War, at Sebastopol, in 1855.

 On reaching the castle gate turn right along an obvious path beneath the castle walls, past a notice board marking the start of the waymarked Mortimer Trail.

The first buildings of the castle passed, after the gatehouse, are the privately occupied Castle Flats.

As the path bears to the left beneath the high walls look up to see the North Range of the castle, much developed and improved by the Mortimers in the early fourteenth century. The most impressive structure of the castle, as seen here from the outside, is the Garderobe Tower which was actually built onto the outside of the Norman walls. Providing extra accommodation for the Mortimers, who entertained lavishly, the tower had eight chambers each with its own garderobe (toilet), an early form of en-suite accommodation. Exactly how medieval castle toilets functioned can be imagined by looking up at the apertures in the outside walls which indicate their positions!

 Follow the path as it bends to the left around the castle walls and begins to descend. Ignore a narrow path coming in sharply from the right but at a Y-junction of paths go right – as indicated by a Mortimer Trail sign. (The path on the left at the junction runs around the castle walls to emerge near Dinham House – see below.) The descent becomes steeper, the path soon reaching a road, through metal barriers.

 Turn left along the road to reach a T-junction. Here turn right to walk out onto Dinham Bridge.

AA. Dinham Bridge

Dinham Bridge was built in 1823 and replaced an eighteenth century bridge which itself had replaced a timber bridge built on stone piers, the latter probably being reused in the eighteenth century structure. The old piers can still be seen just downstream of the current bridge when the river is low. The previous bridge and castle are the subject of a well-known Turner painting of about 1790.

The part of Ludlow known as Dinham takes its name from Joce de Dinan who was granted land here in 1130 when the de Lacy family –

founders of both castle and settlement at Ludlow – temporarily fell out of favour with the Crown. He also held Ludlow Castle for a time during the troubled reign of King Stephen, 1135-1154.

 Turn and walk back across the bridge. At the road junction at the end of it go right. Climb up the road (Dinham) past the site of Dinham Gate to reach St. Thomas's Chapel.

BB. St. Thomas's Chapel

St. Thomas's Chapel, built around 1190, is the oldest building in Ludlow outside of the castle walls. It is dedicated to St. Thomas a Becket, murdered in Canterbury Cathedral in 1170. Derelict by the middle of the sixteenth century it is now incorporated into a later building, and topped by an eighteenth century dovecote. Its single celled interior can be viewed through a large metal grille. The interior roof ribs are particularly fine.

 Bear left at the chapel to continue up Dinham and return to Castle Square, passing Dinham House (on the left) and Dinham Hall Hotel (on the right).

CC. Dinham House

Dinham House is the largest of Ludlow's Georgian mansions and, unusually for the town, is set in spacious grounds. By 1719 it was owned by the Knight family of Downton – see note at Stage 6 – who, in 1748, added two wings to the existing early eighteenth century building. The property later became the town house of the Clive family – see note on Oakly Park in Stage 6 – and their relatives the Earls of Powis. Its main claim to historical fame is that Lucien Bonaparte, brother of Napoleon, lived in it for six months in 1811 – as a prisoner on parole after his capture by the Royal Navy.

Just after passing Dinham House an archway through the castle walls, on the left, leads to a walk around the outside of the castle walls and eventually to the path, taken earlier, from the castle entrance down to Dinham Bridge.

On the right of the road between Dinham House and the Dinham Hall Hotel is a building called The Croft. The name commemorates a former street in the town's medieval grid plan – Christ Croft – which formerly ran north to south hereabouts, approximately where the drive of the Dinham Hall Hotel now runs. It was truncated when the castle and its walls were extended into the north-west of the grid system in the latter half of the twelfth century. There was an Augustinian Friary nearby between 1254 and 1256. It moved to a new site off what is now Friars Walk in the latter year – see note at Stage 7.

DD. Dinham Hall Hotel

A striking late Georgian building erected in 1792 by Samuel Nash, land agent for Richard Payne Knight of Downton Castle. The building, unusual for Ludlow in that it is faced with ashlared masonry, was used as the boarding house of the town's Grammar School between 1894 and the 1970s. Now a luxury hotel. The front of the house (not seen) has a magnificent full-height bow window.

On the right between the Dinham Hall Hotel and Castle Square is Number 2 Dinham which was rebuilt in 1656 after being burned down during the Civil War siege of the town.

 On reaching Castle Square turn right into Castle Street. On the right is:

EE. Castle Lodge

In the sixteenth century this was the home of the Porter, and later the Governor, of the Castle. It has also been a prison in its time. The building has a history going back to medieval times – the surviving arched doorway to the street dates from this time – but was rebuilt in stone in the 1580s, when it was described by Thomas Churchyard as the 'fayre house of Maister Sackford'. Some original panelling of the period survives inside.

The timber-framed upper storey was added later by Robert Berry, like Thomas Sackford an official of the Council of the Marches.

Royalist soldiers were billeted in the building during the Civil War.

The building has more recently been used as a location in the filming of two television series – *Moll Flanders* and *Tom Jones*.

At the Mill Street corner of the building is an old set of stocks. The town stocks and pillory were sited at the top of Mill Street in the seventeenth century.

 Continue along Castle Street and take the first turning on the right – Mill Street. Opposite, at the turning, on the corner of Castle Street and Mill Street are:

FF. The Assembly Rooms

Now used (in part) to house a museum (a successor to that of the Ludlow Natural History Society which was founded in 1833) and the Tourist Information Centre, the Assembly Rooms were built by public subscription and opened in 1840. The cost was £6200 and the architect was a local man, Samuel Stead. As built the premises contained the museum, an assembly room (for balls, concerts and lectures), a supper room, a billiard room, a card room and a reading room.

The ground floor windows facing Castle Street and the mainly glass link to the neighbouring building in Mill Street are modern alterations, and not very sympathetic to the original design.

 Walk down the right-hand side of Mill Street passing, on the right:

GG. The Guildhall

The Guildhall was built by the Palmers' Guild – as its administrative centre – in 1411. A timber-framed aisled hall, it replaced an earlier thirteenth century Guild building.

In 1768 it was re-fronted in brick to a design by Thomas Farnolls Pritchard. Much of the fifteenth century construction remains behind this newer facade however. The asymmetrical position of the Mill Street doorway is a tell-tale clue as to the older building behind the bricks. Inside, an ornate timbered roof is partially obscured by a suspended eighteenth century ceiling.

Next-door to the Guildhall, down Mill Street, the building with the cupola – now called The Coach House – was built in the 1790s by Richard Nash to provide stabling for his large house in Dinham. The jettied cottage next door was split into two dwellings in the 1840s. It contains plaster work of a high quality.

Across the road is:

HH. Number 7 Mill Street

The eighteenth century town house of the Baldwins of Corvedale. Note the initials and date on the old drainheads – 'R.M.B. 1721' – together with a cherub's and one other head on each.

 Continue down to the bottom of Mill Street passing, across the road on the left:

II. The Palmers' Hall of Ludlow College (Old Grammar School)

Another fifteenth century hall of the Palmers' Guild, originally built as a house by a wealthy wool merchant. A Guild grammar school moved to the site in 1527. Taken over by the borough in 1551, after the dissolution of the Guild, the premises are still being used for educational purposes, as part of Ludlow College.

 Reaching the bottom of Mill Street continue past the site of Mill Gate.

Well preserved stretches of the town wall can be seen on either side of the site of the gate.

 Return past the site of Mill Gate and turn right into Silkmill Lane.

Silkmill Lane recalls one of the town's former industries – a silk mill operating hereabouts in the eighteenth century.

 Walking along Silkmill Lane, on the left is:

JJ. Barnaby House

A stone built medieval house, probably originally built around 1300. Traditionally believed to have been used as a hostel by pilgrims travelling to St. Winifred's Well in North Wales, by the fifteenth century it had been converted into a town house for the Barnaby family of Lower Brockhampton. The existing roof seems to date from this period but is thought to have been reused, perhaps originating from a nearby building which was sacked by the Lancastrians after the Battle of Ludford Bridge in 1459. Inside the house a fine Renaissance mural survives, but is not on public display.

Thomas Barnaby was a supporter of the Yorkist cause during the Wars of the Roses, becoming Treasurer to Edward IV. He died in 1471.

In the nineteenth century the house was bought by the grammar school. After a period of use as the school gym it has recently been converted into classrooms for Ludlow College.

 Take the first turning on the left, into Raven Lane.

Formerly 'the Narrow Lane', Raven Lane is a back access lane for the properties on Broad Street and Mill Street.

 Walk up Raven Lane. Go straight across at the crossroads with Bell Lane to view, on the left:

KK. Numbers 14 & 15 Raven Lane

A fine example of a half-timbered building, dating from the second half of the sixteenth century. In 1619 the property belonged to Edward Colbatch, a shoemaker and member of Ludlow Corporation. Well decorated externally, one of its brackets (the lower centre) takes the form of a Sheila-na-gig fertility symbol, although somewhat more restrained than some of its kind!

Not all of Ludlow's buildings are lovingly cared for. Take a look at Number 9 Raven Lane (just below numbers 14 & 15) if it hasn't succumbed to demolition or redevelopment. A great shame as the building is of the same date and pedigree as its fine neighbours.

 Return back down Raven Lane. On reaching the crossroads with Bell Lane turn left. On the left in Bell Lane are:

LL. Numbers 22 to 26 Bell Lane

Unusually for Ludlow, a terrace. Five identical three-storey houses which probably date from the early nineteenth century.

Bell Lane, and its continuation Brand Lane, are cross streets of the original medieval grid plan of the town.

 Walk along Bell Lane to its junction with Broad Street. At the corner on the left at the junction notice:

MM. Oriel House

So called because of its window overlooking Bell Lane. A medieval building much altered in Georgian times. In the fifteenth century it was the Talbot Inn and was the property of the Earl of Shrewsbury.

Wonderful views both up (to the Butter Cross) and down (to Broad Gate) Broad Street from its junction with Bell Lane.

John Leland, writing in 1540, described Broad Street as 'the fayrest part of the town' while Nicholas Pevsner, in 1958, thought it 'one of the most memorable streets in England'.

 Cross Broad Street and turn right to walk down it, to Broad Gate, passing on the way – on the left:

NN. Number 27 Broad Street

Another fine example of the work of the Shrewsbury architect Thomas Farnolls Pritchard who undertook its refurbishment in 1764. The house was originally built in the late seventeenth century for Sir Job Charlton of Ludford, for a time the Speaker of the House of Commons – see the note under Ludford at Stage 6.

 Continue down Broad Street to pass under the arch of Broad Gate and so complete this town trail.

Acknowledgments

This walk could not have been designed nor the book written without the help and kindness of many people and my thanks go out to all of them. My apologies for any omissions below – they are in no way deliberate.

In particular my thanks to:

aRTy Publications – for permission to use the poem *Aymestrey* by R. Tomas.

Val & Steve Bowen – for the warm welcome at the Riverside Inn over the years and during my walking of the route. Also for the transportation.

David Edwards (Heart of Wales Line Travellers Association) – for information regarding Knucklas Viaduct.

Peter Groves (Meridian Books) – for the continuing encouragement and for agreeing to publish this book.

Alan Jones – for the help and company on several stages of the walk, continuing support and tolerance, gate opening skills, and for helping me tell my 'lefts' from my 'rights'.

Sandy McAlear – for test walking parts of Stages 4 and 5.

'Red' and Tom Morrow – for doing the bulk of the test walking....and not complaining!

Gillian Mortimer (Senior Librarian, Ludlow Library) – for research and information on Friars Walk and Bromfield.

Dave and Kerry Walker – for test walking the Ludlow Town Trail.

Maureen Williams (Leintwardine Library) – for research and information on Wigmore Abbey.

'Sam' Williams – for permission to use the photograph on page 127.

Pearl Wright – my sister, for proofreading the initial manuscripts of this book and its predecessor *The Elan Valley Way*.

Frances Yeats/Staff at Leominster Library – for research and information on Wigmore Abbey, Paytoe Hall and Aymestrey Church.

Zog (North Herefordshire Footpath Warden) – for sharing his knowledge of the Rights of Way of the area, advising as to the routing of part of Stage 1, and for the story of 'Dead Woman's Lane'.

Recommended Further Reading

C. Barber, *In Search of Owain Glyndwr*, Blorenge Books, 1998

B. Draper, *The River Teme, from its Source to the Severn*, Brian Draper, Date of publication unknown

G. Hodges, *Ludford Bridge and Mortimer's Cross*, Logaston Press, 1989

G. Hodges, *Owain Glyn Dwr & the War of Independence in the Welsh Borders*, Logaston Press, 1995

D. Lloyd, *Ludlow*, Chalford Publishing Co.,1995

D. Lloyd, *The Concise History of Ludlow*, Merlin Unwin Books,1999

R. Morriss & K. Hoverd., *The Buildings of Ludlow*, Alan Sutton, 1993

P.M. Ray, *Ashford Carbonel - A Peculiar Parish. A Brief History*, P.M. Ray, 1998

M. Salter, *The Old Parish Churches of Herefordshire*, Folly Publications, 1998

M. Salter, *The Castles and Moated Mansions of Shropshire*, Folly Publications, 1988

M. Salter, *The Old Parish Churches of Shropshire*, Folly Publications, 1988

M. Salter, *The Castles of Mid Wales*, Folly Publications, 1991

M. Salter, *The Old Parish Churches of Mid Wales*, Folly Publications, 1991

M. Salter, *The Castles of Herefordshire and Worcestershire*, Folly Publications, 1989

S.C. Stanford, *The Archaeology of The Welsh Marches*, S.C. Stanford, The Old Farm House, 1991

V. Thackeray, *Tales from the Welsh March*, Cressrelles Publishing, 1992

Also by David Milton

The Elan Valley Way

A long distance path loosely based around the course followed by the Elan Valley aqueduct along which Birmingham's water supply has passed since 1905.

The Elan Valley Way starts on the western fringe of Birmingham at Frankley reservoir and ends at the Elan Valley in mid-Wales. It does not aim to slavishly follow the course of the aqueduct but visits many of the more obvious signs of the pipelines on the ground. Although it is never more than about three miles from the line of the aqueduct it takes 128½ miles to do the journey that the aqueduct does in 73½!

The walk, largely following footpaths and bridleways, and with many superb views, passes through some delightful walking areas in the counties of Worcestershire, Shropshire, Herefordshire and Powys. It has been split into ten stages based on the availability of accommodation and public transport and can therefore easily be followed either as a whole ten-day affair or in parts, as time and inclination permit. No section should present any problems for the reasonably fit and there are no prolonged steep ascents.

The book is illustrated with sketch maps and photographs, some of the latter dating from the time when the aqueduct was being constructed.

Price £7.95. ISBN 1 869922 39 5. Paperback. 160 pages.
21 photographs. 21 maps.

Available from bookshops or direct from the publishers (please add £1.00 for post & packing). Send your remittance to:

Meridian Books
40 Hadzor Road, Oldbury, West Midlands B68 9LA